T0339494

INTERPERSONAL SKILLS FOR GROUP COLLABORATION

This lively and engaging text introduces readers to the core interpersonal and organizational skills needed to effectively collaborate on group projects in the classroom and the workplace.

Group projects are critical in preparing students for the realities of today's workplace, but many college students despise group work—often because they have not been prepared with the necessary skills to effectively collaborate. This guide teaches core collaboration skills such as active listening, interviewing, empathy, and conflict resolution. It examines the research and theory behind these skills, and provides tangible ways to practice these skills both alone and in groups.

This guide can be used as a supplementary text for any courses involving group projects, and will also be of interest to professionals in communication, business, and many other fields.

Tammy Rice-Bailey is an Associate Professor of Technical Communication and User Experience at the Milwaukee School of Engineering, USA.

Felicia Chong is a UX Researcher with an academic background in rhetoric and technical communication.

INTERPERSONAL SKILLS FOR GROUP COLLABORATION

Creating High-Performance Teams
in the Classroom and the Workplace

Tammy Rice-Bailey and Felicia Chong

Routledge
Taylor & Francis Group

NEW YORK AND LONDON

Designed cover image: Rawpixel / Getty

First published 2023
by Routledge
605 Third Avenue, New York, NY 10158

and by Routledge
4 Park Square, Milton Park, Abingdon, Oxon OX14 4RN

Routledge is an imprint of the Taylor & Francis Group, an informa business

© 2023 Tammy Rice-Bailey and Felicia Chong

Library of Congress Cataloging-in-Publication Data
Names: Rice-Bailey, Tammy, author. | Chong, Felicia, author.
Title: Interpersonal skills for group collaboration : creating high-performance teams in the classroom and the workplace / Tammy Rice-Bailey, Felicia Chong.
Description: Abingdon, Oxon ; New York, NY : Routledge, 2023. | Includes bibliographical references and index. |
Identifiers: LCCN 2022041965 (print) | LCCN 2022041966 (ebook) | ISBN 9781032259079 (hardback) | ISBN 9781032259062 (paperback) | ISBN 9781003285571 (ebook)
Subjects: LCSH: Interpersonal relations. | Cooperation. | Teams in the workplace.
Classification: LCC HM1106 .R533 2023 (print) | LCC HM1106 (ebook) | DDC 302.3--dc23/eng/20220915
LC record available at https://lccn.loc.gov/2022041965
LC ebook record available at https://lccn.loc.gov/2022041966

ISBN: 978-1-032-25907-9 (hbk)
ISBN: 978-1-032-25906-2 (pbk)
ISBN: 978-1-003-28557-1 (ebk)

DOI: 10.4324/9781003285571

Typeset in Bembo
by Taylor & Francis Books

CONTENTS

FIGURES

ACKNOWLEDGEMENTS

We would like to thank our artist, Leah Fleishman, for her creative depictions of interpersonal scenarios.

In addition, we would like to thank the following individuals for their valuable conversation and support: Brandon Bailey, Kim Baker, Eric Baumgartner, Elaine Carey, Brian Castelli, Sean Daly, Alicia Domack, Brian Eschrich, Annemarie Fleishman, Joshua Hertzog, Tyra Hildebrand, Wendy Leeds-Hurwitz, Deanna Leitzke, Lorelei Parolin, Rachel Schmidt, and Saj Thachenkary.

INTRODUCTION

Quite often, we hear complaints from students that they hate group work. Just as frequently, we hear friends and colleagues criticize their committees or projects that never seem to gain any traction. We believe that with focused attention to interpersonal skills and basic team processes, individuals can not only overcome the disagreeableness associated with such collaborations, but they can also create productive and enjoyable group experiences. *Interpersonal Skills for Group Collaboration: Creating High-Performance Teams in the Classroom and the Workplace* is designed to help individuals, especially those who dread group work, be successful in their group collaborations.

We sometimes think that the problems we see in college-level collaborations will disappear when the students enter the workplace. After all, employees are motivated to perform so that they can retain their jobs and earn a living. So, we might not expect team members to skip meetings, produce substandard work, or miss deadlines. Yet, they do. Some issues that we see in college groups may not be immediately identifiable in the workplace. For instance, it is less likely that a member of a workplace group would try to take charge because there would typically be a project manager who is tasked with the leadership. However, power struggles do exist in workplace teams, particularly in cross-functional teams, where group members may have incompatible expectations or goals.

The practices presented in this text can be used in various types of groups to maximize the effectiveness of its members and to move the collaborative experience from good (or mediocre) to great.

Who should use this book?

This book is intended for use by individuals and teams, both in the college classroom and in the workplace. A great time to use the text is when you are part

DOI: 10.4324/9781003285571-1

of a new team or any time you want to improve your own collaboration skills. The readings and discussion questions will give you ideas to consider, while the activities allow you to actually practice some of the behaviors that make for successful collaborations.

If you are a college instructor, we recommend using this book as a supplementary text in any classroom where you will be assigning group projects. Assign students to read a chapter and then use class time to work through and debrief the discussion questions and to facilitate the activities at the end of that chapter.

If you are a leader, provide this book to your teams at the start of a project or when a group is facing challenges collaborating effectively. Ask members of your groups to read a chapter and its associated discussion questions on their own, then dedicate some time at the start of the next meeting to facilitating the activities at the end of that chapter. Although the chapters do build upon each other, each chapter can stand alone. This means that if you are targeting a specific skill your team is lacking (say, showing empathy), you may decide to have your team members focus on that chapter.

How is this a different approach to group collaboration?

Many contemporary textbooks on teamwork or group collaboration focus on team processes and roles, but they ignore the foundational interpersonal skills that are necessary to function in such teams. This text provides practices that are intended for every group member, regardless of their role in the group. For this reason, the text can be used by individuals, group leaders, and instructors, alike.

While the book is accessible and concise, it is not overly simplified. Our work is grounded in research from various disciplines to show how teamwork can be improved in both the workplace and classroom. We not only draw from recent research in various disciplines, but also our own professional and field experience. This book provides research and practice-based rationale for the practices it describes and includes activities that allow group members to practice the skills it describes.

Why these particular skills?

As authors of this book, we have between us over two decades of corporate experience and almost equal that amount of experience teaching at the university level. We are both interested in team dynamics and parsing out what makes some teams more effective than others. We have conducted pedagogical and programmatic research on such related topics as the interpersonal relationships of technical communicators and subject matter experts, the challenges faced by remote and global teams, and the use of improvisational games to teach interpersonal communication skills to college students.

In our research and discussions with other industry and academic professionals, we have landed on several behaviors that characterize members of strong, productive teams. The majority of these behaviors are interpersonal in nature. A few others involve critical documents and processes. We have grouped these behaviors into eight chapters, which you can easily work through individually or with your groups. The chapters can also be used as supplemental text or as standalone topics to address specific problem areas you (or the teams you facilitate) encounter in your collaborations.

Our goal is to have group members work through these chapters (and the activities contained within them) over a few weeks, honing such skills as listening, practicing empathy, and interacting with their teammates—at the same time that they are working on actual group projects.

Underlying philosophies

The authors of this book have spent several years each as instructors of technical communication (TC). TC emphasizes clarity of message, conciseness of message, and an emphasis on the rhetorical triangle surrounding messages. The **rhetorical triangle** posits that to be effective, a message should take into account the audience at which it is directed, the context in which the message is delivered, and the purpose of the message. We believe these same principles readily apply to collaborative work in teams. In addition, we both have experience working in corporate settings, and from this experience, we have observed helpful ways to think about group work, including emphasizing the intercultural nature of teams and the importance of diversity in teams. Finally, one of us has a background in improvisational theater and has found that many tenets of improvisation work equally well in teams.

Intercultural nature of teams

A reality for American students and workers is that they live in a global economy, where many project teams are composed of members from different parts of the world. This is an important point because our cultural identity impacts the ways in which we experience the world and the ways in which we behave in groups.

Researchers (Mujtaba & Pohlman, 2010) have concluded that working professionals tend to behave according to the way they were socialized within their national culture. This means that even if you are working with an American team, some members of your team may have learned different rules for group behavior based on their native culture. For instance, in both India and Malaysia, a group member who is considered less powerful is expected to show respect to a group member with more power by listening attentively (Roebuck et al., 2016). This is attributed to the high-power distance of those countries. In contrast, in America (a low-power distance culture) it is generally more common for power to be more distributed and for group members to be more direct in their conversation—regardless of their own or others' positions within the group. Chapter 2 provides more information about cultural differences related to listening.

Although this book is written for (and the majority of our experience comes from) North American teams, we realize that most teams are composed of varying amounts of cultural diversity. Dr. Wendy Leeds-Hurwitz, Director of the Center for Intercultural Dialogue, explains, "It is a common mistake to assume that American teams are monocultural. In reality, Americans are a heterogeneous group" (personal communication, December 28, 2021). Leeds-Hurwitz describes how, within the United States, there is no one singular or homogeneous culture. We are composed of many cultures with differing values, beliefs, and behavioral expectations. Understanding the intercultural nature of American teams implies that it is important to understand the intercultural implications related to significant components of successful group collaboration.

Even the most seemingly homogeneous groups are often intercultural in nature. Take, for instance, a group of five students studying at an American engineering school. If each of these students is an 18–20-year-old mechanical engineering major who lives in the dorms, and all of these students are residents of the United States, the group might "look" like it is composed of people from the same "culture." However, unless all members of this group grew up in the same neighborhood, attended the same schools and houses of worship, and shared the same ethnic heritage, foods and music, it is much more likely that even this group is composed of individuals with different cultural identities.

Consider the social media meme of Ozzy Osbourne and King Charles, who share a similar demographic profile. Both are White, British men in their seventies. But that is possibly where the similarities end. One is the unofficial "Godfather of Metal" known for his reality television show, the other served in the Royal Air Force and Royal Navy and has recently ascended to the British throne. Despite their observable similarities, if these two were asked to collaborate on a team, there is little reason to suspect that they would approach the work and challenges in the same way. It is a common misconception that if we look the same (or share some similar demographics), then we must think the same and act the same. Even these few examples demonstrate that this is clearly not true.

Throughout this book, we will point out intercultural and cross-cultural considerations that are specific to the topics contained within each chapter. We also encourage you to do your own research if you will be working on a team made up of members from different countries or backgrounds. But do keep in mind that researchers (Ramasamy, Ling, & Ting, 2007) have also found that as countries become more multicultural, the assumption of national homogeneity might be incorrect. Just as with the US and UK examples provided above, there is typically heterogeneity even within national borders. In other words, just because you and your team members are from different cultures doesn't necessarily mean that you will immediately have conflicting approaches or ideas.

Importance of Diversity

When we organize teams, we look to create groups that are diverse. Diversity often includes differences in gender, age, and ethnic heritage. Other types of diversity commonly seen on teams include differences in educational or professional background. As the authors of *Group Dynamics for Teams* (Levi & Askay, 2021) explain, "differences in knowledge, skills, and perspectives provide a team with a great pool of cognitive and information resources." These differences, they maintain, can lead to better problem-solving and higher quality decisions (p. 268). But diverse groups are not always easy.

One challenge with diverse groups is that they may have to work harder to understand each other. For instance, sometimes group members come from a variety of disciplines, departments, or organizations that use different vocabularies or have different assumptions about what is important or how the world operates. These types of differences may lead to unproductive conflict and take some time and effort to reconcile. This is the paradoxical dilemma of diversity (Bassett-Jones, 2005).

However, any team that suffers from homogeneity of world view, background, or skill sets is prone to the perils of biased decision making. Without diversity, there is a greater chance of **groupthink**, which is the loss of independent thinking and the tendency for group members to arrive at consensus without fully exploring a problem or its potential solutions. In a *Harvard Business Review* article, Emmerling and Rooders (2020) explain that groups of individuals who have potentially opposing points of view can more effectively counter these biases. They further explain that when trying to complete complex tasks that require diverse skills and perspectives, heterogeneous groups often outperform homogeneous ones.

As facilitators, instructors, and participants of group collaboration, our stance is that it is the responsibility of group members to tap into the diversity of their group. This means that each group member should work to offset the likelihood of groupthink by calling attention to the ideas of all group members and working to counterbalance any intentional or unintentional silencing of group members. Such vigilance will help ensure the ideas brought forth by an underrepresented viewpoint have the opportunity to be fully considered.

In our years of teaching groups to collaborate, we've observed that some team members are more comfortable talking, while others prefer to do more listening. This is not necessarily problematic, unless the talkers never listen or the listeners never talk. For a robust conversation, you want all group members to contribute. Even if you are not the group leader, you may (and should!) invite all group members to be heard. For instance, if Carlos has not spoken up much during the last part of the meeting, you could ask, "Carlos, what are your thoughts on this issue?" See Chapter 5 for more tips on how to encourage other team members to actively participate.

Looking for underrepresented viewpoints might also include going outside of your team when you are trying to figure out the perspective of your clients or stakeholders. If you are designing a product for people with mobility challenges, but none of the members of your team fit that description, don't guess. Go in search of such individuals and talk with them.

The most "diverse" group will not benefit from that diversity unless all voices in the group have had ample floor time.

Improvisation and Collaboration

Another atypical aspect of this book is its application of improvisational theater games. As you progress through the text, you will notice that some of our activities make use of improvisation. We believe that improvisation is a perfect companion to collaboration, in that improvisation gives us the opportunity to work on several interpersonal skills that are critical to group collaboration. As such, we would like to provide you with a bit of background on improvisation.

Improvisation (improv) is a type of theatrical performance that is unplanned and unscripted. In a nutshell, improv performers are given a prompt by the audience or facilitator, and the performers have to act spontaneously or react in the moment. Although it may sound like an "anything goes" performance, improv is actually a structured, rule-based performance because it requires each team member to listen, respond affirmatively, and make statements that further the scene or story.

Using improv as a problem-solving activity has been shown to improve team building and creativity. As an innovative acting coach and creator of improv theater games, Spolin (1999) argued that it emphasized the importance of team-work because there is no "right" way to solve the problem. This method is so effective that businesses are calling on improv training centers for help (Scinto, 2014). In fact, in 2017, the University of Chicago Booth School of Business partnered with Second City to bring improv training into the classroom. This partnership is likely to produce both theoretical and practical suggestions for how improv can be used as a tool to achieve collaboration and group cohesion in an academic setting (University of Chicago Booth School of Business, 2017).

So, what are the rules of improv? Comedian Tina Fey (2012) articulates these rules to include: (1) say, "yes"; (2) say, "yes, and …"; (3) there are no mistakes; and (4) make statements. Saying "yes" allows you to accept the reality presented by your partner and to further the scene or story, as your goal is to create a performance based on what your partner(s) are saying or how they are acting. This requires careful listening and the ability to be flexible and collaborative.

Based on recent research on the effectiveness of using improv in the technical communication classroom (Rice-Bailey, 2021), several of the activities we use in this text are based on improvisational theater games. What is important to remember is that saying "yes, and" will not only put you in a mindset that is open to possibilities, but it will also provide you and others on the team the "participative safety" (a concept that we elaborate more on in Chapter 6) necessary for everyone to feel more comfortable and confident about sharing their ideas.

Trust building and participative safety

Team collaborations are most productive when group members trust each other and feel safe that they will not be ridiculed or ignored. For this reason, we refer to both trust and participative safety throughout this text.

According to Covey and Merrill, the authors of *The Speed of Trust* (2006), trust is a "pragmatic, tangible, and actionable asset" and not a soft, illusive quality. Not only does trust build an environment conducive to facilitating candid and productive discussion, but it also directly contributes to the team's success. In fact, Google conducted a research project on teamwork and found that trust is the quality that contributed the most to team success (Bariso, n.d.). We concur that trust is essential in teams and believe that many of the same practices for successful collaboration, which we discuss throughout this book, also result in building trust among team members.

Trust can be built in a variety of ways. When team members are up-front about their motives and ideas, they tend to be trusted by their team members. This "straight talk" (Covey & Merrill, 2006) looks very much like honesty. For instance, if a team member believes that they might be biased against an idea, they could build their credibility by owning up to this. Group members who act with authenticity, transparency, and integrity tend to be trusted. Another trust-building practice that we emphasize on our teams is to give team members the benefit of the doubt. Giving each other the benefit of the doubt makes team members more open-minded and receptive to each other. Providing and asking for this consideration encourages team members to believe that they have only good (and not harmful) intentions. As a bonus, a recent cross-cultural study (Jasielska et al., 2020) found that those who give others the benefit of the doubt are found to be happier, so it's a win–win situation!

When group members trust each other, group members are more likely to experience participative safety. **Participative safety** refers to the comfort with which a team member feels they can share their ideas without being ridiculed or ignored. A safe environment, describes collaboration researcher Delizona (2017), includes approaching conflict as a collaborator (not as an adversary) and replacing blame with curiosity. Research shows that participative safety positively contributes to team creativity (Peltokorpi & Hasu, 2014). In Chapter 5, we discuss being assertive and confident when presenting ideas. However, a group member's confidence will be limited if they do not believe they are in a safe environment. Throughout this text, we provide practices that will help you build a safe environment for your team.

How this text is organized

For purposes of exploration and description, we have organized this book into separate skill-based chapters. However, it is important to note that these skills frequently overlap. This is particularly true of Chapter 9, which details documents and practices that support the other chapters.

Each chapter begins with an introduction to the topic, followed by specific practices related to the topic that are supported by literature from various fields (including communication, psychology, business, theater, and user experience). Next, we provide remote and technological considerations (except for Chapters 8 and 9), with the understanding that since the COVID-19 pandemic, more teams are functioning and collaborating remotely. This is followed by a summary of the chapter and discussion questions that individuals or groups can use to further explore the topic of the chapter. Finally, we present activities that can be implemented in the classroom or in the workplace to give groups the opportunity to engage in specific interpersonal skills. We end each chapter with a list of references. Every feature of the chapter ties into our book's approach and overall goal of helping our readers facilitate effective collaboration in their groups.

We hope you enjoy this book!

References

Bariso, J. (n.d.). Google spent years studying effective teams. This single quality contributed most to their success. www.inc.com/justin-bariso/google-spent-years-studying-effective-teams-this-single-quality-contributed-most-to-their-success.html.

Bassett-Jones, N. (2005). The paradox of diversity management, creativity and innovation. *Creativity and Innovation management*, 14(2), 169–175.

Covey, S. M. R., & Merrill, R. R. (2006). *The speed of trust*. Glencoe, IL: Free Press.

Delizona, L. (2017). High-performing teams need psychological safety. Here's how to create it. *Harvard Business Review*, August 24. https://hbr.org/2017/08/high-performing-teams-need-psychological-safety-heres-how-to-create-it.

Emmerling, T., & Rooders, D. (2020). 7 strategies for better group decision-making. *Harvard Business Review*, September 22. https://hbr.org/2020/09/7-strategies-for-better-group-decision-making.

Fey, T. (2012). *Bossypants*. New York: Little, Brown & Company.

Jasielska, J., Rogoza, R., Russa, M. B., Park, J., & Zajenkowska, A. (2020). Happiness and hostile attributions in a cross-cultural context: The importance of interdependence. *Journal of Happiness Studies*, 22(1), 163–179. https://doi.org/10.1007/s10902-020-00224-w.

Levi, D., & Askay, D. A. (2021). *Group Dynamics for Teams*. Los Angeles, CA: Sage.

Mujtaba, B. G. & Pohlman, R. (2010). Value orientation of Indian and US respondents: A study of gender, education, and national culture. *SAM Advanced Management Journal*, autumn, 40–49.

Peltokorpi, V. & Hasu, M. (2014). How participative safety matters more in team innovation as team size increases. *Journal of Business and Psychology*, 29(1), 37–45. https://doi.org/10.1007/s10869-013-9301-1.

Ramasamy, B., Ling, N. H., & Ting, H. W. (2007). Corporate social performance and ethnicity: A comparison between Malay and Chinese chief executives in Malaysia. *International Journal of Cross Cultural Management*, 7(1), 29–45. https://doi.org/10.1177/1470595807075169.

Rice-Bailey, T. (2021). The benefits of improvisational games in the TC classroom. *Technical Communication Quarterly*, 30(1), 63–76.

Roebuck, D. B., Bell, R. L., Raina, R., & Lee, C. E. (2016). Comparing perceived listening behavior differences between managers and non angers living in the United States, India, and Malaysia. *International Journal of Business Communication*, 53(4), 485–518.

Scinto, J. (2014). Why improv training is great business training. *Forbes*, June 27. www.forbes.com/sites/forbesleadershipforum/2014/06/27/why-improv-training-is-great-business-training/?sh=40679dec6bcb.

Spolin, V. (1999). *Improvisation for the theater: A handbook of teaching and directing techniques*. Evanston, IL: Northwestern University Press.

University of Chicago Booth School of Business. (2017). New partnership with Second City Works and the University of Chicago Booth School of Business to study how improvisation can promote better workplace dynamics. January 31. www.chicagobooth.edu/media-relations-and-communications/press-releases/new-partnership-second-city-works-and-university-chicago-booth-school-business-study-how.

1

ENGAGING IN CONVERSATION

Questions to consider

- What are the potential benefits of engaging in small talk?
- What are some conventions of conversation?
- How do you establish common ground with people you don't know well?
- Why is it important to call your group members by name?
- How can you identify as a group member?
- What are the benefits of face-to-face meetings?

1.1 Introduction

When a team is first assembled, it typically takes some time for individual members to begin to function as a cohesive group. This is because becoming a team is a process. In this "forming" stage, you will begin to build trust and bond with each other. Much of this will initially happen through conversation.

This chapter looks at various elements of conversation. More specifically, it examines conversational practices that can help your group start to coalesce and function as a team instead of as a group of individuals. We begin this chapter with a discussion of small talk because it is one of the first activities in which you will engage as you are getting to know your teammates.

1.2 Practices for engaging in conversation

The following practices related to conversation will help your group begin to function as a unit.

DOI: 10.4324/9781003285571-2

1.2.1 Initiate small talk

Before your group meetings start, you might find yourself alone with one or more group members. In such situations, consider making small talk with those group members. **Small talk** is casual conversation in which you exchange information on superficial topics, such as the impending snowstorm, the poor Internet connectivity at the cafe, or how tight the seats are on the airplane. Making small talk can set a friendly tone for your meeting.

The National Communication Association (2012) gives advice for encouraging students to make small talk and notes that "small talk is a powerful instrument for beginning a relationship." Small talk typically begins with someone making a comment or asking a question. For instance, if your group is meeting in an office that overlooks the city, you might state to the group member sitting next to you, "What a great view!" If you are meeting online, and you and another teammate sign on a bit early, you might ask that person how the weather is in their part of the country. You could even comment on the jersey they are wearing. If one of your teammates is wearing a Green Bay Packers' jersey, you might say, "Great season your team is having. Too bad about Watkins's injury."

In some situations, you may know your group members, but in others, the group members may be strangers to you. Psychology research (Sandstrom & Boothby, 2021) shows that people tend to avoid having conversations with strangers, due to worries that include not enjoying the conversation, not liking their conversation partners, and not being able to carry out the conversation. However, research (Schroeder, Lyons, & Epley, 2021) also shows that these fears or concerns are often misplaced because those who *do* try to talk to strangers often end up having a positive experience. In fact, while "chit-chat" may seem meaningless, it serves many purposes.

In her book *We Need to Talk: Conversations That Matter*, National Public Radio host Celeste Headlee (2017) writes that conversations are one of the most foundational skills people can learn. As she explains, "So much hinges on what might seem like trivial chats" (p. xv). And yet, as Headlee posits, as a society, our conversation skills have eroded, and we regularly miss opportunities to have in-depth dialogue. In fact, we have discovered that many full-blown conversations evolve from simple small talk. Additionally, small talk allows you to connect with others and even enjoy working with them. When you join a new group, think of small talk as a way to open the door to more meaningful conversations.

Mastering the art of small talk can lead to expected opportunities. Take, for instance, the chance conversation between two coworkers, Susan and Tia (11Alive, 2021). The two women discovered that both of their husbands were in renal failure and needed a kidney donation. Unfortunately, neither woman was a match for her husband's kidney type. However, during their conversation, each woman discovered she *was* a match for the *other*'s husband. You guessed it, each became a kidney donor to the other's husband. Without this chance conversation, the lives of two separate men might still hang in the balance.

Many organizations have also recognized the value of small talk. Moon (2017) emphasizes the importance of planning for small talk in the workplace. She describes a conversational activity used by employees at the tech firm Trello, called Mr. Rogers. For those of you who have never seen his television show, Fred Rogers was a children's television personality who was well-known for encouraging children to have confidence in themselves and to be neighborly toward each other. The Mr. Rogers activity used by Trello randomly pairs employees from different teams and, using the same spirit of inquiry demonstrated by Mr. Rogers, has them engage in a 15-minute conversation. This activity allows employees to socialize with others whom they might not otherwise interact with. Moon notes that the Mr. Rogers activity has been one the most successful social programs for 65% of their remote teams.

In our classes, we have used a similar activity, which we call Coffee Talk. This activity was developed because we noticed that some of our student project groups were not as cohesive as we would have liked, particularly during and immediately following the COVID pandemic. We were looking for a way to address the issues that students didn't know each other very well and they were already feeling isolated. In this activity, we randomly pair one student with another, and have the two classmates share a 10-minute walk (during class time). If they want to grab coffee together, we encourage that, but it's not necessary. We repeated this activity each week during the first five weeks of class, so that each student has a personal conversation with five of their classmates. The Coffee Talk activity is described in further detail at the end of this chapter.

Initiate small talk to get to know your team members.

1.2.2 Engage in conversation

One you start to work with your group members, your conversations will become more substantial. You will still engage in small talk, but you will also have the opportunity for deeper and longer conversations. In fact, engaging in conversation will be the primary method by which you get to know your team members. This is why conversation is the topic of this first chapter.

We are not the only ones who see the value of conversation. Employers concur. Ortiz, Region-Sebest, and MacDermott (2016) conducted a survey of US employers asking them which oral communication skills are important to company success. Their results show that employers ranked the "ability to engage in conversation" as one of the most valued oral competencies for new hires as a factor in company success. In fact, the 2021 report of the National Association of Colleges and Employers lists verbal communication as one of the top ten skills employers' look for on a candidate's resume (National Association of Colleges and Employers, 2021). One of the reasons employers may value conversation, is that they may be aware that conversation is also a conduit to producing new knowledge. Think about it. If your team is cross-functional or composed of students with different majors or backgrounds, you (and your teammates) will necessarily learn about concepts or processes that are not standard in your department or discipline.

In fact, many business ideas are the result of either planned or impromptu conversations. Consider the example of one of our students who parlayed some theoretical discussions with a colleague into a business opportunity. Jonathan, a User Experience (UX) major, was interning at a start-up company during his sophomore year of college. He hit it off with one of the senior engineers, Max, who took an interest in Jonathan's application program interface design (UX work). During both work-related and casual conversations, Jonathan and Max discovered they had a mutual interest in generative computer technology and natural language processing. Jonathan describes how they would talk "very meta or philosophically" about topics such as how artificial intelligence will transform computing, or how context models in web applications relate to mental models. At one point, they realized that they could create a company that answered one of their questions. The idea for their business was born.

By conversations, we are referring to both in-person and online (via technology) conversations. It just so happens that Jonathan and Max's conversations were entirely online, but many similar types of conversations take place in-person. In fact, some lament that more conversations aren't happening in person. For instance, Sherry Turkle, sociology professor at MIT and author of *Reclaiming Conversation*, argued that we are using technology to communicate with others on a superficial level, but it doesn't yield the same impact as having real-time conversations, which allow us to empathetically connect with others (Turkle, 2016). Virtual or online conversations can allow you to empathetically connect with others, but they may take more time and effort.

Whether in-person or virtual, groups often do not take advantage of conversation and subsequently lose opportunities to strengthen their relationships. Headlee (2017) writes that these lost moments and the lack of time and effort we make to understand those around us have taken a toll on society. We concur with Headlee and thus consider conversations and conversation skills to be integral aspects of group collaboration.

Having conversations not only helps build team relationships but also produces knowledge.

1.2.3 Review conventions of conversation

What if conversation is not your strong suit? Even if you are not a big conversationalist, reviewing the basic rules of conversation will help. A popular social skills group for teenagers on the Autism spectrum (PEERS, 2021), breaks down conversation into a few specific actions. This program focuses on the process of trading information and highlights the (often unspoken) rules of conversation. We find that these conventions apply to almost any conversation and suggest even neurotypical group members use them to become better conversationalists:

- Ask the other person about themselves.
- Answer your own question (so that you are *answering* as well as *asking* questions).
- Find common interests.
- Share the conversation (what we call give and take).
- Don't be an interviewer (be sure to *answer* as well as *ask* questions).
- Don't get too personal at first.
- Assess the other person's interest.

As you can see, finding common interests is one of the rules (or conventions) of conversation. Finding common interests is oftentimes also the *goal* of trading information. The idea is that common interests are the foundations upon which many relationships are formed. Finding common interests will provide you with topics to talk about and potentially activities you can engage in together. Other conventions of conversation include give and take and establishing common ground, which are covered later in this chapter.

The conventions of conversation rely on give and take, a mutual exchange, where participants take turns having or yielding the floor to each other. In a conversation, the person who is speaking is said to "have the floor." In general, you will take the floor once you have been signaled it is appropriate to do so—either when another group member stops talking or when they ask a question. "Holding the floor" is when someone signals to others that they are not yet ready to stop talking. For instance, if you are in the process of telling a story and pause to recall a specific detail, the pause might signal to the group that it is someone else's turn to talk. However, if you do not want to yield the floor (because you want to finish the story), you might elect to insert a verbal cue, such as "um" or "ah." This signals to your group members that you are not ready to yield the floor.

As parents and teachers of school-aged children know, conversation is an acquired skill. We know several youngsters (and not-so-youngsters!) who would be great conversationalists if they would ever yield the floor. Instead, some of them have become experts in holding the floor and sharing each thought that crosses their mind. The PEERS training we previously mentioned advises that during a conversation, not only should you be mindful of monopolizing the conversation, but you should also allow the other person to talk and not interrupt them. We emphasize this point because conversations are a give-and-take that offer you the opportunities both to learn and to express.

Conversations are about learning; if you monopolize the conversation, you are unlikely to learn much. One way to think about this is to consider the amount of speaking and the amount of listening you generally do in a given situation. If you are talking less than 25% of the time, ask yourself if you are contributing enough to the conversation. If you're talking 75% or more, consider what might be different about the conversation if you talked less and listened more.

Yielding the floor might be difficult for those who are accustomed to carrying the conversation, but be mindful of how often and how long you hold the floor during a conversation.

If you are talking the majority of the time, ask yourself what you are learning from the conversation.

1.2.4 Establish common ground

Another convention of conversation is to establish a common ground. **Common ground** is the belief that you share opinions, interests, or experiences with another. Finding common ground with your team members enables you to establish and develop relationships with them. It also allows you to appreciate them as a complex (and hopefully rational!) individual. This appreciation will come in handy in battling the natural skepticism we often feel toward people and groups with which we are unfamiliar. In Chapter 6, we will examine creativity in groups and discuss how skepticism is a part of human nature.

Research in psycholinguistics and social psychology shows that people gravitate toward common ground because it makes them feel more socially connected and "better about themselves" (Fast, Heath, & Wu, 2009, p. 905). Another study (McKinley, Brown-Schmidt, & Benjamin, 2017) shows that common ground can not only promote efficient communication but also promote memory retention of conversation, thereby facilitating future conversation. In other words, establishing common ground can not only improve your communication, but also your personal well-being.

When you encounter new team members, you may be cautious or hesitant about working with them, but don't let these initial reactions stop you from getting to know them. Instead of writing these individuals off and resigning yourself to working with people you may not have chosen, consider attempting to build common ground with them. Finding common ground with your team members will help you start to build team cohesion. **Team cohesion** is the feeling of connectedness you feel with your team. Already having established some common ground will also help you to work together in a collaborative way to resolve any issues that arise down the road, when you have inevitable disagreements.

In the collaborations we have facilitated in the workplace and in the classroom, we have discovered some best practice for establishing common ground with others. These include the following:

- Avoid asking seemingly innocuous questions that you may perceive to be conversation starters but may actually make the other person uncomfortable. For example, if you ask your classmate who has a different accent than yours,

"Where are you from?" and they answer, "Michigan," avoid asking the follow-up question of, "Where are you *really* from?" If your intention is to build common ground, you want to talk about topics that make you similar, not what makes you different. In our experience, if someone feels comfortable sharing their home state or country with you, they will disclose it themselves. Figure 1.1 shows another example of how *not* to start a conversation.

• Ask follow-up questions based on what others are disclosing. If your team member shared that she broke her leg last week, you can ask her follow-up questions on how she is feeling or how she broke her leg. However, if your team member shared that he was in the hospital last week, it would be more appropriate to ask, "How are you feeling now?" than to ask, "What were you in the hospital for?" The second question might be considered intrusive.

• Ask questions based on your mutual/current setting. For example, if you are talking to team members in your communication class, you can begin the conversation by asking, "Is this your first communication class?" or "Are you a communication major?" Other common topics include the bag or backpack they are using, any sports-team related attire they are wearing, or photographs they put in their office (e.g., of their pets, vacations, or family).

Focus on finding common ground with your team members.

FIGURE 1.1 What not to say to a team member

1.2.5 Call people by their names

It is important that you get to know and use the names of your group members. Referring to a team member as "Amir" instead of "him" is not only more professional, but it also confirms to Amir that you care enough to learn and use his name in conversation. When you meet your group members, make a note of their names (jot them down in your notebook or phone) and use their names when you are talking with or about them.

The importance of calling team members by name often comes up in the beginning of a semester, when students are asked to give group presentations. Countless times, we have heard students refer to something one of their teammate's stated earlier in the presentation (which we applaud!) by stating, "As *he* said …" (which makes us cringe). Our feedback to students who refer to their teammates as "he" or "she" is to please refer to the student by name. When students don't refer to a group member by name, we get this uneasy feeling that perhaps they don't know the person's name, which is problematic. You need to know the names of all of your group members. Not knowing someone's name is far less common in the workplace, but we have occasionally been jarred when workplace team members refer to others on their team by "he" or "she." It's simply unprofessional.

In the classic text, *How to Win Friends and Influence People*, Dale Carnegie (1964) emphasizes the importance of remembering and using someone's name because to that person, their name "is the sweetest and most important sound in any language" (p. 47). As long-time educators, we know the importance of remembering student names, as it has often been considered an inclusive teaching practice. One study (Cooper et al., 2017) conducted in a large-enrollment undergraduate biology course shows that such a practice positively impacted student attitudes about the course, where students felt more valued in the course and more invested in the course. Students also indicated that they would feel more comfortable reaching out to the instructor and more confident in their performance in that class if their instructor knew their names.

Similarly, research in the workplace confirms the significance of knowing and using your team members' names. For example, one study (Douglas et al., 2021) shows that surgical caps displaying medical staff's names and roles can indeed improve effective communication in the operating room. It certainly lessens the chance that the wrong person will answer to "you."

Remember and call your team members by their names.

1.2.6 Identify as a group member and use "we"

Identifying as a group member means that when you talk about the work of the group, use the term "we." To build group cohesion, choose to talk about your work as a team instead of your individual contributions to the team. For example, in one workplace study of flight attendants, the researchers found that employees who were primed with the social identify prime (using "we") showed an "increased willingness to engage in coordinated team action compared with those who received a personal identity prime" (Ford, O'Hare, & Henderson, 2013, p. 499). Once again, this shows how important it is to be mindful of your word choice.

In both the classroom and the workplace, we have regularly provided feedback counseling individuals to use the term "we" when discussing the work or accomplishments of the team. Just as referring to a team member as "he" or "she" can make the group appear to be a disjointed group of individuals, so too does talking about "my" individual work on a project. The better options are to use actual names and the word "we." In both cases, the result is an increase in the actual and perceived cohesion of the group.

Identifying as a group member has other benefits. It can also make you perform better. A number of educational research studies (e.g., Chen et al., 2021; Edwards, Barthelemy, & Frey, 2022; Wilton et al., 2019) indicate that students' sense of belonging impacts their academic performance: Those who feel that they belong perform better. In addition, there is a large body of research (e.g., Greenaway et al., 2015; Sandstrom & Boothby, 2021) that shows a positive correlation between a person's sense of wellbeing and them identifying as a member of some group.

Use the term, "we" instead of "I" when talking about the work of the group.

1.2.7 Choose face-to-face channels

When we work on teams, there are times that we need or want to exchange information with other group members outside of the established meetings. For instance, if your team is engineering a prosthetic limb and one of your teammates is researching a competitor's product, you might want to share with that person some online information you discovered about defects in that competitor's product. In this situation, you are very likely to text or email your teammate a link with a brief explanation. However, while this approach may be the "quickest," it is not often the most productive.

Although it may seem "time consuming" or "too much effort" to collaborate and communicate in person, don't underestimate the productivity and efficiency it brings. In one study that Turkle (2016) describes, college students were asked to communicate in four ways: face-to-face, video chat, audio chat, and online instant messaging. When their degree of emotional bonding in these modes were assessed, the results clearly show that face-to-face conversations led to the most emotional connection, and online messaging led to the least.

When you send a chat or e-mail message, you are missing the opportunity for a (potentially robust) discussion that could occur in a face-to-face encounter. The amount of context you can provide in a brief e-mail is limited, and your team-mate may quickly skim the information and reject it. Even if you were to send a lengthy email that contained your reasoning behind forwarding this link and explaining exactly how you thought it could help them accomplish their task, the information could ultimately end up lost. Why? Because business emails are not intended to be long, and if it is long, your teammate will likely skim it. Addi-tionally, the context you provide may not resonate with your teammate, whose focus is likely different from your own.

Consider what might have happened if you had picked up the phone and called, video-conferenced, or even met with your teammate in person. A con-versation (as opposed to a one-directional message) would give you the chance to provide details about why you thought this information would be helpful. It would also allow your teammate to ask you specific questions about the infor-mation you found and how you saw it fitting into their work. Another, possibly more important, benefit to a conversation is that (even if it is fairly brief) it could lead to discussing other, possibly related topics. Again, had you simply sent an email, this second, serendipitous conversation and the value gained from it would not have occurred.

Furthermore, we recommend face-to-face channels whenever possible because it is harder to detect the tone of your language when communicating via texts or emails. We have both received seemingly "angry" emails from other team members or colleagues that we later realized we incorrectly interpreted because of the tone of the email.

Face-to-face communication often results in the strongest emotional connection.

1.3 Remote and Technological Considerations

One of the greatest losses that remote and virtual teams encounter, particularly in the post-COVID workplace, is the lack of opportunities for casual "water cooler talk." **Water cooler talk** is conversation that spontaneously occurs when colleagues happen upon each other at common gathering spots such as the water cooler or the photocopy machine. Water cooler talk helps to build and maintain relationships. It is also where an organization's unofficial network (or grapevine) gets its sustenance. In addition, there is research that suggests engagement in water-cooler talk results in a new employee being

> more well-liked, rated as having higher job competence, more likely to be recommended by co-workers for future tasks or projects, and more likely to receive helping behavior from co-workers than new employees who engage in low levels of private interactions.
>
> (Lin & Kwantes, 2015, p. 254)

That's a lot of benefit to lose when your team is meeting virtually.

In fact, even research (Fisher & Bennion, 2005) from the early 2000s, when there was an increased move to telecommuting (or working from home), suggests that the absence of face-to-face time with one's colleagues can result in lack of sense of community. Researchers (Larbi & Springfield, 2004) explain that we were so eager to trade in cubicles for electronic communication that we "underestimated the impact and necessity of physical reality" (p. 102). What this suggests is that whenever possible, we consider the possibility of physically spending time together. We recognize that this is not always an option, but it is a goal to strive toward.

Research (Rice-Bailey, 2014) suggests that one method to recreate the benefits of water cooler talk (particularly, building and maintaining workplace relationships) is to dial into a conference call early to take advantage of small talk. You could similarly connect a bit early to a video conference. Another way to stay connected to your team members is to connect via professional social networking sites such as Linked In, where you can learn more about your team members and communicate congratulations on promotions and work anniversaries. Yet another option is to make small talk a regular part of each meeting. Frisch and Greene (2021) suggest that even though many suffer from Zoom Fatigue and possibly bristle at the idea of planning for "noncritical" talk, small talk should be included in the meeting agenda.

1.4 Summary

This chapter explains the following key points about becoming a team:

- Use small talk as a way of getting to know your team members.
- Practice conventions of conversation to ensure an adequate give and take of information.
- Establish common ground or common interests by asking questions about others.
- Call people by their names to be inclusive and professional.
- Identify as a group member and use the word "we" when talking about the group.
- Choose to communicate in person whenever possible.

1.5 Discussion questions

1. Do you know of any good conversationalists? What do they do that makes them good?
2. What are some ways you have started conversations with group members? Be specific. What did you say or do?

3. When you are in a group, how much talking do you do? Do you usually wait until everyone else has spoken up, or do you initiate the conversation?
4. Can you think of any situations in which you chose to send a text or an e-mail to a group member that might have been more successfully handled in a face-to-face meeting or phone call?

1.6 Activities

1.6.1 Coffee talk

This activity can be done in person or online. In this activity, group members are randomly assigned a partner with whom they will engage in a 15-minute non-project-related conversation.

Object: The object of this activity is to give group members the opportunity to have a personal conversation with another member of their group. This allows both group members to not only practice the art of conversation, but also to learn more about each other.

Setup: If the group is in person, the pairs should have a private 15-minute talk and might even go on a walk to have this conversation. Online, the pairs should be given their own breakout rooms so that they can focus on their conversation.

Activity: The pairs should have a 15-minute conversation about any topic(s) they like EXCEPT anything related to their project or group. The idea is to get to know the other person. If either of the two notice the conversation ever drifting to the group or project, they should make a conscious effort to steer the conversation in another direction.

Debrief: The pairs can share with the larger group the types of topics discussed by the pairs, but this (or any formal debrief) is unnecessary. Again, the idea of this activity is to simply learn more about another group member.

Take-away: Spending some time getting to know your team members on an individual level will help you build relationships with them.

1.6.2 Transcribing a conversation

Prior to this activity, each group member will record and transcribe an actual conversation between two people they know and that takes place outside of the group.

Object: The object of this activity is to show group members that verbal communication is much more complex than it might initially appear.

Setup (on your own): You will record a conversation that happens outside of the group. To do this, you will need to select two family members or friends who don't mind being recorded for about 15 minutes. Follow these instructions:

1. Tell the two people you are interviewing that the recording has begun (then start the recording on a mobile phone or other device). **Important note**: Using a voice-to-text tool will make this activity a bit easier. However, if you only have the ability to record voice-to-audio, you will need to take the additional step of listening to a portion of the recorded conversation and typing up what is being said.

2. Encourage the two to have a "normal" conversation about anything that interests them. Interact very little (if at all) with the people being recorded (the more people who are talking, the more difficult the transcription will be).

3. After about 10 minutes, stop the recording.

4. Later, listen to the recording looking for about two minutes' worth of dialogue that best represents what you consider to be a "typical conversation" (this is generally a little bit into the recording, once the participants have gotten past the novelty of being recorded).

5. Once you have selected a section of the conversation to transcribe, try to capture (in writing) this part of the conversation. Include what was said, by whom and in what order. Also make note of any pauses or interruptions that occur during this piece of conversation.

   - If you recorded the conversation using a voice-to-text feature, simply select 1–2 minutes of conversation from the transcript to focus on. Add initials (of the speakers) to the transcript to indicate when the next person was speaking. Also indicate on the transcription where there were pauses or overlaps in the talking.
   - If you recorded the conversation using a voice-to-audio feature, listen to the recording and select 1–2 minutes of conversation to focus on. Type out exactly what is being said and indicate (with initials) who is speaking. Also indicate where there were pauses or overlaps in the talking.

Activity:
After the group members transcribe their respective sections of conversation, they should be placed into groups of three to share their transcriptions with each other and answer the following questions as a group:

1. How did you record the conversation: voice-to-text or voice-to-audio?
2. What was the most difficult part of the transcription process?
3. What did this activity teach you about conversation? *Example: (When they are in a conversation, people often interrupt each other)*

Takeaway: When you take the time to transcribe a conversation, you will see that within a conversation, there are many things going on simultaneously. For instance, people often interrupt or talk over each other, and people often do not complete their thoughts.

References

11Alive. (2021). Chance conversation leads to lifesaving kidney donations [Video]. You-Tube, May 27. www.youtube.com/watch?v=wrfnRrjYAcM.

Carnegie, D. (1964). *How to win friends and influence people*. Simon & Schuster.

Chen, S., Binning, K. R., Manke, K. J., Brady, S. T., McGreevy, E. M., Betancur, L., Limeri, L. B., & Kaufmann, N. (2021). Am I a science person? A strong science identity bolsters minority students' sense of belonging and performance in college. *Personality & Social Psychology Bulletin*, 47(4), 593–606. https://doi.org/10.1177/0146167220936480.

Cooper, K. M., Haney, B., Krieg, A., & Brownell, S. E. (2017). What's in a name? The importance of students perceiving that an instructor knows their names in a high-enrollment biology classroom. *CBE Life Sciences Education*, 16(1). https://doi.org/10.1187/cbe.16-08-0265.

Covey, S. M. R., & Merrill, R. R. (2006). *The speed of trust: The one thing that changes everything*. Simon & Schuster.

Davey, L. (2019). Let your team have that heated conversation. *Harvard Business Review*, December 23. https://hbr.org/2019/12/let-your-team-have-that-heated-conversation?autocomplete=true.

Douglas, N., Demeduik, S., Conlan, K., Salmon, P., Chee, B., Sullivan, T., Heelan, D., Ozcan, J., Symons, G., & Marane, C. (2021). Surgical caps displaying team members' names and roles improve effective communication in the operating room: A pilot study. *Patient Safety in Surgery*, 15(1), 1–27. https://doi.org/10.1186/s13037-021-00301-w.

Edwards, J., Barthelemy, R. S., & Frey, R. F. (2022). Relationship between course-level social belonging (sense of belonging and belonging uncertainty) and academic performance in general chemistry 1. *Journal of Chemical Education*, 99(1), 71–81. https://doi.org/10.1021/acs.jchemed.1c00405.

Fast, N. J., Heath, C., & Wu, G. (2009). Common ground and cultural prominence: How conversation reinforces culture. *Psychological Science*, 20(7), 904–911. https://doi.org/10.1111/j.1467-9280.2009.02387.x.

Fisher, L. & Bennion, L. (2005). Organizational implications of the future development of technical communication: fostering communities of practice in the workplace. *Technical Communication*, 53(3), 277–288.

Ford, J., O'Hare, D., & Henderson, R. (2013). Putting the "we" into teamwork: Effects of priming personal or social identity on flight attendants' perceptions of teamwork and communication. *Human Factors*, 55(3), 499–508. https://doi.org/10.1177/0018720812465311.

Frisch, B. & Greene, C. (2021). Make time for small talk in your virtual meetings. *Harvard Business Review*, February 18. https://hbr.org/2021/02/make-time-for-small-talk-in-your-virtual-meetings.

Greenaway, K., Haslam, S. A., Cruwys, T., Branscombe, N. R., Ysseldyk, R., & Heldreth, C. (2015). From "we" to "me": Group identification enhances perceived personal control with consequences for health and well-being. *Journal of Personality and Social Psychology*, 109(1), 53–74. https://doi.org/10.1037/pspi0000019.

Headlee, C. (2017). *We need to talk: How to have conversations that matter*. HarperCollins.

Larbi, N. E. & Springfield, S. (2004). When no one's home: Being a writer on remote project teams. *Technical Communication*, 51(1), 102–108.

Lin, I. Y., & Kwantes, C. T. (2015). Potential job facilitation benefits of "water cooler" conversations: The importance of social interactions in the workplace. *The Journal of Psychology*, 149(3), 239–262. https://doi.org/10.1080/00223980.2013.874322.

McKinley, G. L., Brown-Schmidt, S., & Benjamin, A. S. (2017). Memory for conversation and the development of common ground. *Memory & Cognition*, 45(8), 1281–1294. https://doi.org/10.3758/s13421-017-0730-3.

Moon, L. (2017). The surprising cognitive benefits of small talk at work. *Trello*, June 26. https://blog.trello.com/surprising-cognitive-benefits-of-small-talk-at-work.

National Association of Colleges and Employers. (2021). The key attributes employers seek on college graduates' resumes. Press release, April 13. Retrieved from www.naceweb.org/about-us/press/the-key-attributes-employers-seek-on-college-graduates-resumes/.

National Communication Association. (2012). Instructor's corner: The art of small talk. February 1. www.natcom.org/communication-currents/instructors-corner-art-small-talk.

Ortiz, L. A., Region-Sebest, M., & MacDermott, C. (2016). Employer perceptions of oral communication competencies most valued in new hires as a factor in company success. *Business and Professional Communication Quarterly*, 79(3), 317–330. https://doi.org/10.1177/2329490615624108.

PEERS. (2021). Worksheet. Marquette University. www.marquette.edu/psychology/marquette-autism-project/.

Rice-Bailey, T. (2014). Remote technical communicators: Accessing audiences and working on project teams. *Technical Communication*, 61(2), 95–109.

Sandstrom, G. & Boothby, E. J. (2021). Why do people avoid talking to strangers? A mini meta-analysis of predicted fears and actual experiences talking to a stranger. *Self and Identity*, 20(1), 47–71. https://doi.org/10.1080/15298868.2020.1816568.

Schroeder, J., Lyons, D., & Epley, N. (2021). Hello, stranger? Pleasant conversations are preceded by concerns about starting one. *Journal of Experimental Psychology: General*, 151(5), 1141–1153. https://doi.org/10.1037/xge0001118.

Turkle, S. (2016). *Reclaiming conversation: The power of talk in the digital age*. Penguin.

Wilton, M., Gonzalez-Niño, E., McPartlan, P., Terner, Z., Christoffersen, R. E., & Rothman, J. H. (2019). Improving academic performance, belonging, and retention through increasing structure of an introductory biology course. *CBE Life Sciences Education*, 18(4), ar53. https://doi.org/10.1187/cbe.18-08-0155.

2

LISTENING

Questions to consider

- Why is listening important to group collaboration?
- What should you do before offering a solution in a group setting?
- What are the four types of noise that can interfere with your ability to listen?
- What are some typical distractions to listening, and how can you avoid them?
- What does it mean to listen to what is *not* being said?
- What is the relationship between non-judgmental and critical listening?
- What are effective responses to compliments?

2.1 Introduction

Are you a good listener? How do you know? Perhaps you are careful to "take the floor" during only half of the conversation. But simply not talking does not mean you are effectively listening.

Listening is more than just hearing. Listening is a process that also involves attending (or paying attention) to what you are hearing, deciphering the meaning of that message, evaluating the message, remembering it, and then responding to it. Lapses or interference can occur at any point during this process. In addition, various other factors can get in the way of your ability to effectively listen to your groupmates.

Listening is a critical collaboration skill. Listening should not be a passive act. Effective, engaged listeners are a critical ingredient in any conversation. Not only does listening help you to understand your group members, but it also allows you to solve problems together. Subsequently, listening is foundational to completing the work of the group. In fact, employers consistently rate listening among the most important workplace skills (Kluger & Itzchakov, 2022). However, the

DOI: 10.4324/9781003285571-3

importance of listening in the communication process is often overlooked, and many people receive little to no training on how to listen effectively. While high schools, colleges, and universities often provide students with the technical skills that will help them be successful in the workplace, there is less emphasis on interpersonal skills such as listening.

In this chapter, we provide you with practices that will help you to remove barriers to effective listening.

2.2 Practices for listening

In our academic and workplace experience, we have identified several listening practices that are especially beneficial in a group setting. However, it is important to realize that what is considered effective (and even polite) listening differs from culture to culture.

In **low-context cultures**, the meaning behind verbal messages is found within the words that are being spoken, while in **high-context cultures**, the meaning of a message is dependent upon the context (or situation) in which the message is delivered. These concepts were originally developed by Edward T. Hall in *The Silent Language* (1959) to explain how cultures could affect communication. Researchers (Roebuck et al., 2016) explain that listeners in low-context cultures (such as the United States) are encouraged to explicitly state what they mean, while listeners in high-context cultures (such as India and Malaysia) are taught to pay attention to the implicit meanings of messages. In cross-cultural groups, the two styles may conflict and group members may become frustrated with or insulted by the styles of others in the group. It is always important to educate yourself on the prominent listening style of the group with which you are working. For instance, before working on a team with Malaysian group members, you might research the phrase "polite listening Malaysia." For more information on the multicultural considerations of team communication, see the *Introduction* of this book.

Following are listening practices we have used in American classrooms and meeting rooms.

2.2.1 Listen first

Respected and effective group members know the benefit of listening first, or what author of *The 7 Habits of Highly Effective People* Stephen Covey (2004) calls "seek first to understand." Time and time again, we have witnessed group members who move their team forward by listening before they expect to be listened to.

We are not the only ones who advocate listening first. Mediation expert William Ury (TedxTalks, 2015) talks about a time when Venezuelan president Hugo Chávez leaned in close and proceeded to shout at him for about a half hour. Instead of trying to defend himself, Ury simply nodded and listened. Eventually, Chávez's shoulders slumped, and he asked Ury what he should do. Ury noted that because he listened to Chávez, Chávez was willing to listen to him. According to Ury, "Listening may be the golden key that opens up human relationships."

This does not mean that you should refrain from speaking up in the meeting until everyone else has spoken. In fact, some research suggests that the first person to speak in a meeting is often perceived as the group leader (Anderson & Kilduff, 2009). In psychology, this is known as "cascade effects" where group members tend to follow the suggestions or ideas of those who spoke or acted first (Sunstein & Hastie, 2014). However, we advise offering a solution only after you have listened to what other team members have to say.

Before you take a position or offer a plan of action, listen to what your team members are saying and weigh their viewpoints with your own. When you listen to their ideas, you will be able to point out natural places of overlap with your own ideas. Listening to their ideas also allows you to anticipate potential reservations others might have about your ideas. This will enable you to adjust your message accordingly. For instance, let's say you intend to advocate for the use of a particular online meeting platform. Before pitching your idea, you listen to what other team members have to say about the various platforms, and you discover that one of your teammates does not like the platform you intended to recommend because of its poor video quality. Knowing her specific reservations will allow you to be more effective in your bid because you can acknowledge and address them.

In meetings, speak up early (and often). However, before making grand proclamations or offering full-scale solutions, take the time to listen to your teammates.

2.2.2 Minimize "noise"

Various types of "noise" can interfere with the listening process. One type of noise, which communication scholars refer to as **psychological noise**, involves allowing your current beliefs or ways of thinking to interfere with your ability to fully listen to another. For instance, if you hold specific political or religious views, and you are listening to someone with opposing views, you may spend some of your listening energy mentally debating with what the other person is saying instead of trying to fully understand them. If your team member is suggesting that the team use a specific software application to keep track of your project plan, and you can't stop thinking about how much trouble you've had with that application in the past, you are probably not fully open to what your teammate is suggesting because you are experiencing psychological noise.

One way to deal with psychological noise is to try to recognize when you have an emotional reaction to another's ideas. Ask yourself if this reaction might be the result of any biases you hold, and then challenge yourself to listen despite this bias. Another way to intercept psychological noise is to put aside your preconceived ideas as others are talking. As Brian Castelli, vice president of business development for Luminate Health, explains:

Of course you will have your position, but keep an open mind when you enter a conversation. Have the courage to admit when another idea is better than yours. Ultimately you want to do what is best for the organization.

(Personal conversation, March 27, 2022)

Other types of noise include **physical noise**, which refers to any sound outside the people who are communicating (think, a blaring siren or a jackhammer); **physiological noise**, which refers to any barriers within the people communicating (hearing or visual impairments, for example), and **semantic noise**, which describes listening problems that can occur because of the different meanings each of you attribute to a word. For instance, let's say that during a group meeting, a team member approaches a topic that you feel is beyond the scope of your project, and you suggest moving the new topic to a *parking lot* of related, but not critical information. If the member who initially raised the topic thinks that a parking lot is a place where ideas go to die, but you think a parking lot is a place for later consideration, then you are experiencing semantic noise, that is interference based on how the two of you define a certain term. You can see how semantic noise might be a source of misunderstanding. Figure 2.1 shows another example of semantic noise.

FIGURE 2.1 Example of semantic noise

Take steps to mitigate the various types of noise that negatively impact your ability to fully listen to your teammates.

2.2.3 Avoid distractions

When we are coaching groups, we often need to emphasize the importance of being present in the moment. Typically, this conversation stems from observing team members who are attempting to multitask during a group meeting.

Being present in the moment or exhibiting "mindfulness" (Good et al., 2016) is important for a couple of reasons. First, when you allow yourself to be distracted during a conversation, the person with whom you are talking may feel slighted or become irritated. Think about the group member who is constantly checking their cell phone or working on another project while you are meeting. The second problem with allowing yourself to be distracted is that you will likely miss information that the other person is giving you. Research shows that multitasking is largely a myth (Rosen, 2008), as it impairs our cognitive task performance (Wang & Tchernev, 2012).

It is especially important for group members to be present and fully engaged during team meetings. One way to avoid typical distractions during a meeting is to make them unavailable. When you are meeting your team members in person, turn your phone off or put it away. Turkle (2016) argues that the mere presence of a phone on the table (even a phone turned off) changes what people talk about. Because we fear that our conversations may be interrupted, we keep them light. Other studies (Canale et al., 2019; Tanil & Yong, 2020; Ward et al., 2017) show that the mere presence of your phone affects your cognitive ability by causing "brain drain" or problems with memory recall. In other words, although your phone may be a useful communication tool, it can negatively impact your productivity when working with your team.

If you allow your devices (or anything else) to distract you, you might miss critical information (both verbal and nonverbal) that is being communicated. Additionally, allowing yourself to be distracted might communicate to some group members that you don't consider the meeting important enough for your full attention.

Note taking, which is a form of active engagement, has long been shown to help us remember important/key points. Research (e.g. Bohay et al., 2011) shows that note taking also helps college students develop a deeper understanding of the texts that they are studying. We have found that note taking also allows us to focus on the conversation at hand. However, the way you take notes makes a difference. Some studies (e.g. Mueller & Oppenheimer, 2014) suggest that when listening, taking notes on a laptop is less effective than taking notes longhand. To help avoid distractions in your meetings, try taking notes longhand, using pen and paper.

When you are in a meeting, put your phone away, remove your ear buds, and take notes.

2.2.4 Listen beyond what is being said

Effective listening often involves depth listening. **Depth listening** is listening to what people say (with their words, their tone, and their bodies) and trying to ascertain any deeper meanings that lie behind these messages.

In addition to listening to what your team members are saying, practice "listening" to their nonverbal messages. To do this, watch for specific cues, like someone shifting in their seat to indicate that they want to move on, take the floor, or wrap up. Chapter 3 provides more detail about conveying and reading nonverbal messages. Depth listening involves listening both to what people say and what they do *not* say.

When listening to teammates, also listen for what they are *not* saying. Sometimes there is an issue that is affecting the entire group, but no one wants to address it directly. Because no one mentions or discusses this "elephant in the room," there may be an underlying sense of anxiety that affects the project. Other times, what is not stated might be some difficulty that an individual group member is experiencing. They may spend time talking about superficial issues while ignoring deeper, underlying issues.

When listening to our group members, we find it helpful to ask ourselves, "What are they not saying?" This question has helped us identify underlying issues that team members are intentionally or unintentionally avoiding. For example, we had a team member who was smart and hardworking, and his work was consistently accurate. However, because he never talked about his interactions with the client, we started to wonder how he was making decisions without the client's input. Our observation that he was not talking about the client led one of us to ask this team member what the client thought about the data. Our team member was surprised that he was expected to be keeping the client informed of his progress, but quickly understood the importance of doing so. If we had not made the effort to listen to what this teammate was not saying, we might never have recognized or corrected this error in the group's process.

Listen to what is being said and what is not being said.

2.2.5 Listen non-judgmentally, then critically

Effective listening involves both nonjudgmental and critical listening (Devito, 2019). Our first responsibility as a listener is to try to understand the message we are receiving. To do this effectively, we need to listen non-judgmentally, with an open mind. Our second responsibility as a listener is to evaluate what the message means to us or to our project. We do this by critically analyzing what we have heard. After that, we determine if and what type of a response is warranted.

Non-judgmental listening is similar to the concept of saying "Yes, and ..." that we covered in the *Introduction* to this book. Non-judgmental listening is listening without any particular expectations or bias. It is accepting a message that is given to us without overly simplifying or complicating it. It is also important not to interrupt your team members while they are in the middle of sharing their ideas. We may ask questions while listening non-judgmentally, but they are typically clarifying questions that we ask to gain more information from the speaker. For example, if a teammate suggests a plan to redesign our stainless-steel product using rubber, we may be initially opposed to the idea for several reasons. But as a listener, it is our first responsibility to quiet our own biases so that we can actually understand our teammate's idea. We should allow our teammate to explain her idea and perhaps ask her questions to clarify our own understanding. For this reason, we might ask, "Are you saying the entire widget would be made of rubber, or just the handles?"

Once the teammate has answered any questions that have arisen about her idea and we are confident that we have understood the idea, we can begin to discuss its merits and shortfalls. Critically examining ideas does not only mean challenging them, but also means exploring ways to modify, strengthen, or implement these ideas.

In our teaching experience, we have found that sometimes students have trouble listening because they can't move beyond their preconceived notion or fundamental belief of what is "good" or "better." In these cases, we like to remind students that when they are listening to others, they should try to focus less on what they themselves think is "right" or "true" and more on what is best for the team or the project. For example, one student may want to use Microsoft Word to write their group recommendation report because they are most familiar with it, but another team member suggests using Google Docs because of its collaborative ability. The important point here is that neither application is intrinsically better than the other, and the team members should make decisions on what makes sense for the project and the team, not what they themselves prefer.

Listen first to understand an idea and second to refine it.

2.2.6 Provide targeted feedback (and compliments)

In the groups that we facilitate, feedback and feedback mechanisms are important listening tools. The challenge is that not everyone knows how to provide targeted feedback. This is where we take a page from the writing workshops we have facilitated. When we teach group members to provide feedback to each other, we focus on moving beyond the ubiquitous and not-always-helpful "good job!"

Providing targeted feedback to your group members is one way to be an effective listener. You might wait until a group member stops talking or politely interrupt them and ask if you can paraphrase or summarize what they have said. As we explain in Chapter 5, it is important to not only be able to summarize your ideas, but also to summarize what you have heard from others. This is especially critical during brainstorming sessions, where you want to ensure that you have captured all ideas. You might say something like, "Let me see if I understand your idea …" or "What I am hearing you say is …" It is helpful to be able to summarize someone's idea before you offer an evaluation of it.

When you like a team member's idea, make an effort to tell them! In our experience, many team members don't naturally compliment each other, or if they do, they provide vague praise such as, "Good idea," or "I agree." In our classroom and corporate experience, we have found complimenting others is not only an exceptional method for reflecting and providing feedback on their ideas, but it also creates a rapport with that group member. Instead of offering general praise, try offering a specific compliment such as, "That's a great idea because it allows us to expand our solution and come in under budget."

It is just as important to accept compliments in a modest and graceful way. Sometimes, when we compliment students' work, they don't accept the compliment. Instead, they respond with something like, "It was nothing" or "Thanks, but I didn't do anything special." Here are some ways we recommend responding to compliments:

- "Thanks for noticing."
- "I appreciate your compliment. It means a lot to me."
- "I put a lot of effort into this project, so it's great to be recognized."

As we noted in Chapter 1, bragging about oneself can often backfire, but giving sincere compliments to another is proven to improve your team members' collaborative experience. In fact, one study (Cheon, 2016) found that verbal compliments are found to have a greater impact on job attitudes than getting a promotion or increased compensation!

When providing feedback, move beyond, "I agree with you" and give sincere compliments.

2.3 Remote and technological considerations

Despite your best efforts to listen, staying focused during an online meeting can be difficult! Especially if your camera is off and you are not the meeting facilitator, it's natural for your thoughts to wander during an online meeting. When you recognize that you're no longer listening, try to return your attention to the call. Gershman (2020) recommends having a pad of paper nearby so you can jot down any intrusive thoughts that are interfering with your ability to listen. Getting these thoughts out of your head and onto paper will allow you to return your attention to the meeting and attend to the non-related issues afterwards.

In an online meeting, we usually recommend that those who are not the active speaker mute themselves to not interrupt the speaker with their background/physical noise (e.g., dogs barking, children playing, or speakers echoing). More importantly, we have found that muting ourselves until the speaker is done conveying their point or finishing their thought prevents us from intentionally or unintentionally cutting the speaker off, as it is usually not possible for two to speak at the same time (unlike in an in-person setting). Muting yourself actually enables you to be a better listener.

2.4 Summary

This chapter explains the following key points about listening skills in group collaboration:

- Before offering full-scale solutions, take the time to listen to your teammates.
- Take steps to mitigate the various types of noise that negatively impact your ability to fully listen to your teammates.
- Listen both to what is being said and what is not being said by your group members.
- Listen first to understand an idea and second to refine it.
- Put your phones away and keep them turned off when having in-person conversations with your team members.
- When providing feedback, move beyond, "I agree with you," and give sincere compliments.

2.5 Discussion questions

1. What are some practices you can use to avoid psychological noise?
2. Besides putting away your mobile phone, what other things can you do to make sure that you are not distracted in a conversation or meeting?
3. How difficult is it for you to listen non-judgmentally?
4. When was the last time that you received positive feedback from others? How did it make you feel?
5. Do you regularly give compliments to your teammates? Why or why not?

2.6 Activities

2.6.1 Recreating what you hear

This activity can be done either in-person (with partners sitting with their backs to each other) or online (with video turned on, but the drawings being described out of sight).

Object: This activity asks group members to listen closely and ask clarifying questions in the process of recreating a drawing.

Setup: This activity is done in pairs. Before the activity begins, each group member should find a simple black and white drawing that they can explain to

another group member. These images can be hand drawn or selected from online images. Each person should also have a blank piece of paper and a pencil.
   Activity:

1.   Each partner should have selected a simple drawing and have that drawing in front of them (so they can accurately describe it) but kept out of the view of their partner.
2.   Partner A should begin by describing their drawing to Partner B.
3.   Partner B should attempt to recreate the drawing based on their partner's description. While they are drawing, partner B should be encouraged to ask clarifying questions of their partner.
4.   After three minutes, start round two. In round two, the partners switch roles. Partner A will now attempt to recreate what Partner B describes.
5.   After both rounds are complete, partners should compare their recreated renderings to the original images and notice how similar (or dissimilar) they are.

Post-activity discussion questions:
   When you were describing the image:

1.   How did you ensure that your instructions were clear?
2.   How helpful were the questions asked by the drawer?

When you were drawing:

1.   What did your partner do that was helpful in your task?
2.   Which of your partner's instructions were difficult to follow?

   Take-away: Listening closely often includes asking clarifying questions so that you can better understand what the speaker is describing.

2.6.2 Rewind

This activity can be done in either an online (e.g., in Zoom's gallery view) or an in-person (standing in a circle) setting.
   Object: The object of this activity is to listen critically, make connections between disparate ideas, and then retrace the origin of those ideas.
   Setup: To prepare for this activity in person, group members should stand in a circle (or, if online, decide the order in which the speakers will go) and be prepared to listen to what the person before them said.
   Activity:

1.   Once the group is standing in a circle or being arranged online in the gallery view, the first person starts by saying any word (for example, "red").

2.   The person to their left (or the next person in line) should say a word that the initial word could connect to (for example, "balloon").

3.   The next person (to their left) should consider only the word that was immediately spoken ("balloon") and say a word that connects with that word (for example, "carnival").

4.   Go around the circle (with each person making a connection to the previous word) two times.

5.   Have the last person who spoke turn to the previous person (the person on their right) and state why they chose their last word (for example, "I said blue because you said ocean").

6.   Have the previous person turn to the person on their right and state why they chose their last word (for example, "I said ocean because you said wide").

7.   Continue to "rewind" the circle until participants have vocalized the reasoning behind all of their word choices.

8.   Repeat 1–7, so that you effectively do the activity twice.

Post-activity discussion questions:

1.   How easy or difficult was it to think of a word that related to the word before yours?

2.   How easy or difficult was it to recall why you chose the word you did?

3.   Did this activity become easier the second time? Why or why not?

Take-away: Critical listening allows us to see connections between disparate ideas and to make decisions based on these connections.

References

Anderson, C. & Kilduff, G. (2009). Why do dominant personalities attain influence in face-to-face groups? *Journal of Personal and Social Psychology* 96(2): 491–502.

Bohay, M., Blakely, D. P., Tamplin, A. K., & Radvansky, G. (2011). Note taking, review, memory, and comprehension. *The American Journal of Psychology*, 124(1), 63–72. https://doi.org/10.5406/amerjpsyc.124.1.0063.

Canale, N., Vieno, A., Doro, M., Rosa Mineo, E., Marino, C., & Billieux, J. (2019). Emotion-related impulsivity moderates the cognitive interference effect of smartphone availability on working memory. *Scientific Reports*, 9(18519).https://doi.org/10.1038/s41598-019-54911-7.

Cheon, Y. (2016). The effects of compliments on the feelings of job attitudes of hotel employees. *International Review of Management and Marketing*, 6(3), 584–589.

Covey, S. R. (2004). *The 7 habits of highly effective people: Restoring the character ethic.* Free Press.

Devito, J. A. (2019). *The interpersonal communication book.* Pearson.

Gershman, S. (2020). Stop zoning out in Zoom meetings. *Harvard Business Review*, May 4. https://hbr.org/2020/05/stop-zoning-out-in-zoom-meetings.

Good, D. J., Lyddy, C. J., Glomb, T. M., Bono, J. E., Brown, K. W., Duffy, M. K., Baer, R. A., Brewer, J. A., & Lazar, S. W. (2016). Contemplating mindfulness at work: An integrative review. *Journal of Management*, 42(1), 114–142. https://doi.org/10.1177/0149206315617003.

Hall, E. T. (1959). *The silent language*. Fawcett Publications.

Kluger, A. N. & Itzchakov, G. (2022). The power of listening at work. *Annual Review of Organizational Psychology and Organizational Behavior*, 9, 121–146. https://doi.org/10.1146/annurev-orgpsych-012420-091013.

Mueller, P. A., & Oppenheimer, D. M. (2014). The pen is mightier than the keyboard: Advantages of longhand over laptop note taking. *Psychological Science*, 25(6), 1159–1168. https://doi.org/10.1177/0956797614524581.

Roebuck, D. B., Bell, R. L., Raina, R., & Lee, C. E. (2016). Comparing perceived listening behavior differences between managers and non angers living in the United States, India, and Malaysia. *International Journal of Business Communication*, 53(4), 485–518.

Rosen, C. (2008). The myth of multitasking. *The New Atlantis: A Journal of Technology and Society*, 20, 105–110.

Sunstein, C. S., & Hastie, R. (2014). Making dumb groups smarter. *Harvard Business Review*, December. https://hbr.org/2014/12/making-dumb-groups-smarter.

Tanil, C. T., & Yong, M. H. (2020). Mobile phones: The effect of its presence on learning and memory. *PloS One*, 15(8), e219233–e219233. https://doi.org/10.1371/journal.pone.0219233.

TEDxTalks. (2015). The power of listening [video]. YouTube, January 7. www.youtube.com/watch?v=saXfavo1OQo&ab_channel=TEDxTalks.

Turkle, S. (2016). *Reclaiming conversation: The power of talk in the digital age*. Penguin.

Wang, Z., & Tchernev, J. M. (2012). The "myth" of media multitasking: Reciprocal dynamics of media multitasking, personal needs, and gratifications. *Journal of Communication*, 62(3), 493–512. https://doi.org/10.1111/j.1460-2466.2012.01641.x.

Ward, A., Duke, K., Gneezy, A., & Bos, M. W. (2017). Brain drain: The mere presence of one's own smartphone reduces available cognitive capacity. *Journal of the Association for Consumer Research*, 2(2), 140–154. https://doi.org/10.1086/691462.

Zenger, J., & Folkman, J. (2016). What great listeners actually do. *Harvard Business Review*. July 14 https://hbr.org/2016/07/what-great-listeners-actually-do.

3

CONVEYING AND MONITORING NONVERBAL CUES

Questions to consider

- What is nonverbal communication?
- What can you do to alter the physical restrictions of your meeting place?
- What do specific nonverbal cues suggest about your group members?
- What nonverbal cues can you use to let your group members know you are open to their ideas?

3.1 Introduction

When we interact with others, we gather information not only from what they say to us, but also from sensory information we exchange with them. We might observe, for instance, a slight grimace accompanying someone's encouraging words. Perhaps we notice the ostentatious clothing they are wearing. We might even make note of the strong fabric softener on their clothing or the squeaking or clicking their shoes make when they are walking away. Each of these is a type of nonverbal communication. **Nonverbal communication** is information a person conveys without the use of language. Nonverbal communication is conveyed through means such as facial expressions, body position, physical gestures, and tone of voice.

Nonverbal messages also include those messages provided by someone's body, clothing, hairstyle, cologne, bag or briefcase, and other "props" (e.g., coffee mug, water bottle, notebook). Each of these messages presents a mechanism through which others interpret or judge you. According to research conducted by Mehrabian (1981), a psychology professor from UCLA, 55% of our communication is non-verbal. Although more recent studies argue that Mehrabian's numbers were

DOI: 10.4324/9781003285571-4

exaggerated, we can say with certainty that when you are working in a group, you will encounter many categories of nonverbal messages.

A major category of nonverbal messages you and your group members engage in constitute what popular culture often refers to as "body language." In the news or in online communities, we see references to the body language of celebrities or politicians. Undoubtedly, you have probably seen social media posts about how to determine someone's attitude from their body language. The scientific term for body language is kinesics.

Kinesics is the study of body movement and gestures associated with nonverbal communication. Valuable information is communicated through kinesics. Kinesics is what you communicate to others through your body movement and gestures. So, how you position your arms is kinesics. Your raised eyebrow is kinesics. Your pointing at the door is kinesics. Kinesics are typically discussed (though not named!) when someone is being coached on job interviewing strategies. Advice such as "make eye contact" and "appear interested" involve someone's body and face and therefore constitute kinesics. An awareness of your own and others' kinesics is important when you are working in a group.

3.2 Practices related to nonverbal communication

The following section describes several nonverbal practices that are important in group collaboration.

3.2.1 Create your own round table

You may be familiar with the image of King Arthur's round table. King Arthur is famously known for using a round table to seat important lords to show that they were equal because no one was seated at the "head" of the table. Therefore, the round table is "a motif intrinsically identified with egalitarianism among its members" (Bornschein, 2013, p. 47). We like the image of the egalitarian round table and consider it critical for group collaboration.

Seating arrangements do have an impact on how groups collaborate. Some classrooms and office spaces are ideal for group work. They are roomy and set up with one or more round tables that allow and foster interaction among all team members. Other spaces are less amenable to collaboration. Think about the rows of desks or tables in some classrooms, where a row constitutes a group. Often in our teaching (and less frequently in our industry work), we have encountered rooms that are set up with immovable tables or desks or other configurations where group members cannot see each other. These setups often hinder the group.

When the room setup is less than optimal for collaboration, there are measures you can take to recreate the feeling of the round table. For instance, if you are in a group of five people sitting in a row of desks facing the front of the room, you can rearrange the desks in a circle, with all group members facing inward. If the desks or tables do not move, you can purposefully position your body to best approximate a round table and suggest that others do the same. How do you do this? Simple. If you have five group members, all facing forward, have the middle person acts as the center point. This center point slides their chair back a few feet. The people to the left and right of the center slide their chairs back slightly and turn their chairs and body toward the center. The people on the ends simply turn their chairs and bodies toward the center. As Figure 3.1 shows, the result is a sort of semi-circle.

Creating a center point minimizes the number of people who have a back to them and subsequently decreases the likelihood that any group member will feel left out. This formation also ensures that group members will have a line of sight with each other. Research (Fernandes, Huang, & Rinaldo, 2011) shows that seating arrangements such as a semi-circle or a U-shape will not only promote eye contact but also improve social interaction between students and instructors. More specifically, round tables were found to support collaborative and student-centered learning activities (Brooks, 2012). For these reasons, creating a round table environment is one of our top recommendations for group collaboration.

In addition to placing your chair in a deliberate way, you should be mindful about the position of your body. As we have explained, it is a good idea to position yourself so that you can make eye contact with all members of your group. You will also want to be mindful of your posture. Recent research suggests that our body posture impacts our thoughts and others' perceptions. For example, high power poses, defined as expansive body postures such as standing tall with the chest out and the hands on the hips, are shown to elevate self-esteem (Körner, Petersen, & Schütz, 2019). Conversely, if your body posture is restricted (e.g., sitting uncomfortably with hanging shoulders, hands crossed, and legs closed), you may be seen as less "agentic" and even less communal then someone who is in a power posture (Abele & Yzerbyt, 2021).

Pay attention to your position and your body when communicating with your team members.

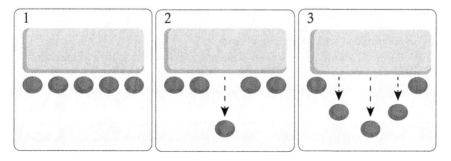

FIGURE 3.1 Positioning group members around a center point

3.2.2 Make eye contact

Another common type of nonverbal communication is eye communication. **Oculesics** is the study of eye communication that includes the frequency, duration, and direction of eye contact.

When it comes to nonverbal communication, oculesics serves many important functions. In a group setting, eye contact can be used to show attentiveness. When a group member is talking, your eye contact with them communicates that (at least on some level) you are engaged with them and are open to hearing more from them. Eye contact can also be used to gain someone's attention. For instance, if the group is assigning a specific task, and you look at a particular group member, you might be signaling them to volunteer. Additionally, eye contact can compensate for physical distance. As Devito, the author of *The Interpersonal Communication Book*, explains, "By making eye contact, you overcome, psychologically, the physical distance between yourself and another person" (Devito, 2019, p. 144). For these reasons, and because many believe that direct eye contact suggests interest, honesty and regard, we encourage direct eye contact between group members.

By looking into their eyes, we might even be able to read if someone in our group is experiencing an emotional reaction to something we or another group member is saying. Research shows that our pupils react to environmental and auditory emotional stimuli. One experiment shows that the pupils dilate during both emotionally negative and positive stimuli, which means our autonomic nervous system is sensitive to highly arousing emotional stimulation (Partalla & Surakka, 2003). In this sense, the eyes really might be the window to the soul!

However, you should be aware that some groups or cultures in the United States vary on their responses to eye contact. Devito (2019) points out that in many Hispanic cultures, direct eye contact suggests equality, and so someone wanting to express respect might avoid direct eye contact with someone of authority. There are also individual differences when it comes to eye contact. In our experience with both workplace and student groups, some individuals are more comfortable making eye contact than others. Eye contact can also mean various things, especially given cultural and neurodiversity. Just because someone doesn't look you in the eye, does not mean they are uninterested or lying. It might mean that they are extremely uncomfortable with the topic or that they are uncomfortable with direct eye contact.

We know of a fifth grader whose elementary school principal cited his inability to make eye contact as "proof" that he was lying. In fact, the child's discomfort with eye contact was a sign of neurodiversity—in this case Autism Spectrum Disorder (ASD). Because the principal was unaware of this diagnosis and clearly knew little about the manifestations of ASD, she erroneously attributed a negative reason to the child's lack of eye contact. This is another reason we do not advocate for trying to find "signs" of deception, when there may be cultural, neurological, or other reasons for a person's behaviors.

When you are talking to your group, attempt to alternate your eye contact among each of your group members. Conversely, when you are listening, try to make regular (but not prolonged!) eye contact with the group member who has the floor. In addition to making an effort to maintain eye contact with your group members (particularly when they are speaking), monitor the eye contact of your group members. Some may be inclined to avoid direct eye contact. If the person consistently lacks eye contact, it could be general discomfort with eye contact. However, if a person only sometimes avoids eye contact, they may be signaling anything from disengagement to disagreement. In this type of situation, you might address the person by name and ask what their thoughts are on the topic at hand. For instance, if during a group meeting in which you are discussing budget, Alexa suddenly stops making eye contact with other group members, you might address Alexa directly by asking, "Alexa, what are your thoughts on the budget?"

Show respect and attentiveness by making eye contact.

3.2.3 Smile

Our facial expressions often communicate our emotions, although the research is mixed on how accurately we can read or interpret such expressions. Simply put, relying on someone's facial expressions alone will provide you with limited information about their mental or emotional status.

Smiling is an example of a facial expression that could be fraught with ambiguity. Some researchers differentiate between "real" and "fake" smiles. For instance, Devito (2019) explains, when we perceive a smile to be authentic, we respond positively; whereas, when we perceive a smile to be fake, we infer that someone is being polite or perhaps deceptive. But people smile for many different reasons. Smiles can indicate friendliness, but they can also indicate embarrassment or sheepishness. For instance, you might smile while apologizing to someone. A smile can also show assertiveness. A boxer may smile at his opponent in a show of dominance. In this sense, reading the meaning behind a smile may not be easy and is definitely dependent on context. Smiles also have a cultural component, and not all cultures view smiles in the same way. As Krys et al. (2015) point out, although numerous psychological studies suggest that smiling individuals are perceived favorably in Western societies, some cultures, such as Japan, India, Iran, and South Korea, may perceive a smiling person as less intelligent than a person with a neutral expression.

Perhaps because they associate smiling with weakness, some people (even in cultures that view smiling in a positive light) are reluctant to smile at others. Think about Instagram or Snapchat photos of celebrities who want to look *hip* and *cool*. *Elle*, a popular women's magazine, even published a list of notorious non-smiling celebs (Elle, 2020). Non-smiling, fierce expressions are purposeful and relay messages like, "don't mess with me," or "I'm not approachable." However, when you are in a group, the message you want to send to your group members is that you are open and amenable to their ideas. Smiling can indicate you are approachable and open to conversation with your group members.

In Western societies, such as the United States, a common way to express openness and approachability is to smile. Research (Krumhuber et al., 2008) suggests that smiling is also positively associated with ethos and competency. Who doesn't want to be considered trustworthy and competent by their team members? Not only will a friendly smile indicate you are approachable, smiles are also infectious. As Barnett (2015) advises, "the act of smiling itself can lift our [own] and others' moods. Whether or not the resistance to smiling is cultural, not smiling, with its attendant mouth and jaw tension, can engender feelings that are the antithesis of joy" (p. 19).

Smiling can show that you are agreeable and open to ideas.

3.2.4 Check the nod

When you are speaking, and I nod, do you assume I am agreeing with you? I might be agreeing with you, but I might not. My nod could signal my agreement with you, or it could signal something else. In Western culture, people's nodding could indicate a confirmation, but it could also indicate that they are still "following" you. This is the reason we might verify the actual meaning of the nod with our group member. It is not necessary to clarify all nodding behavior, but if you are trying to gauge acceptance of your idea, calling out the nodding can be effective. For instance, if Juanita is nodding while I introduce the idea of extending the meeting, I might simply state, "Juanita, I see you are nodding." Then, I might ask her, "Does this mean you agree we should continue?"

Just as body position can influence your self-confidence, so can nodding *when you are speaking*. As Briñol and Petty (2003) found, if you nod while you are speaking, you will have more confidence in what you are saying. It is also likely that confidence will extend to your group members' attitude toward you. That is to say, that when you nod while talking, you build your ethos and your group members may have more confidence in what you are saying. This is in line with another study showing that instructors who use beat gestures (a quick flick of the hand) and head nods in their video lectures have a more positive impact on student engagement and learning (Pi et al., 2022).

Give nodding a try when you are speaking to group members and see if they engage more fully with you.

3.2.5 Use hand gestures

A person's hand gestures, when they precede or accompany verbal information, give us additional information about the person's thoughts. Besides providing more information about a speaker's thoughts, gestures can actually change a speaker's thoughts. It's almost as if the gestures are the physical equivalent to thinking out loud. Our hand gestures also reflect our emotions. There is a large body of research (e.g., Clough & Duff, 2020) showing that hand gestures play an important role in communication and cognition. For example, one study (Vicario & Newman, 2013) shows there is a direct link between our emotions and gestures.

Goldin-Meadow and Alibali (2013) found that encouraging a speaker to gesture has the potential of changing how people think about a problem. These researchers also discovered that using hand gestures further establishes the speaker's credibility. This suggests that people who are confident in their gestures are perceived as knowing what they are talking about. When you are speaking to a group, use hand gestures to emphasize your points. Across languages and cultures, the right side is conventionally associated with positivity or "good things," and the left with negativity (Casasanto & Jasmine, 2010). Try using your right hand to emphasize positive points.

It is important to note that gestures are largely culture dependent. For example, it may be common for North Americans to point using our index finger, but pointing to a person with the index finger is considered impolite in countries like Malaysia.

As you can see, there are plenty of reasons to reinforce your messages with hand gestures! Just be sure the gestures do not have negative connotations with the members of your group.

Using hand gestures is a powerful way to get your point across.

3.2.6 Limit your use of haptic communication

People also communicate by touch. The study of touch or tactile communication is referred to as **haptics**. When someone places a hand on your arm or taps your shoulder, this is haptic communication. Haptic communication can be used to show authentic feelings and emotions such as affiliation, bonding, and loyalty. Studies on the effects of tactile communication show that physical touch can improve mood levels, reduce stress, and even cognitive control (Saunders, Klawohn, & Inzlicht, 2018).

Shaking hands, which constitutes a typical greeting in North America, remains one of the most common examples of touch seen in public and in the workplace. Think about different handshakes you have exchanged. Have you made assumptions about an individual based on the firmness or length of their grip? Studies show that strong grips indicate extraversion while weak grips indicate shyness (Chaplin et al., 2000), and prolonged handshakes of three seconds or more may cause the recipient anxiety (Nagy et al., 2020).

Since the COVID pandemic, we have noticed that some people are still hesitant to shake hands. In a recent survey (Dragomir, Farcas, & Şimon, 2021) of college students, participants indicated that post-COVID, they will use more facial expressions (e.g., raising eyebrows and blinking) than touching as a form of interpersonal communication. This finding is also supported by a similar study in Germany (Matschke & Rieger, 2021), where the majority of the college students surveyed said they do not want to go back to pre-COVID greeting forms (e.g., handshakes and social kissing) due to the fear of contracting the disease. While it is still unknown if current attitudes toward handshakes will revert to pre-COVID practices, we suggest that you limit your use of haptic communication until you are more certain of your team members' preferences and levels of comfort.

The acceptance and use of haptics, or touch communication is highly dependent on culture, and even in a "contact culture," such as the United States, individuals' reactions to touch vary. On some types of teams, for example sporting teams, haptics is an essential form of communication. Consider a football team. Coaches and team members routinely pat each other on the back or backside, and sometimes even express joy by bumping chests with each other. In fact, one study on NBA players found that physical touch such as high fives and fist bumps can "enhance group performance through building cooperation" (Kraus, Huang, & Keltner, 2010, p. 749).

In an office or classroom setting, the use of haptics is much more limited. In fact, the media is filled with politicians, celebrities, and members of the general public who have been outed as predators who include in their arsenal of assaults, inappropriate and unwanted touch in the workplace. Unfortunately, such stories bring negative attention to the topic of touch in schools and the workplace. Largely as the result of such actions and the resulting negative press attention, the current social climate in many Western cultures, including the United States, is to shy away from an unnecessary touch.

Limit your use of touch in the classroom and the workplace.

3.2.7 Observe mirroring

Have you ever been engrossed in a conversation and suddenly noticed your body or hand position is identical to the person with whom you are speaking? Such synchronized movements are referred to as **mirroring**. Mirroring is quite common, and researchers have found that when people interact, there is often a synchronization of their nonverbal behaviors. Such synchronization can typically be seen in people's posture, head movements, hand gestures, leg positions, and facial expressions.

As playwright and coach, Gina Barnett (2015), notes, the result of this synchronization is a feeling of rapport and alignment. This feeling, explain researchers Ashton-James and Chartrand (2009) "cues convergent thinking by signaling a social opportunity for collaboration" (p. 1036). Effectively, if you mirror someone, you are showing them that you are open to them and their ideas. Similarly, if someone mirrors you, they are likely to be empathizing with you and are open to you.

In your groups, you will have the opportunity to observe and engage in mirroring behaviors. In your group conversations, be aware of times that you or others are mirroring another group member. It is quite likely that two group members who are mirroring each other are either in agreement about a point or are engaged in each other's ideas.

An added benefit of mirroring is that it has been found to increase the opportunities for a person to be liked or accepted (Meza-de-Luna et al., 2018)!

To build feelings of rapport and likability, look for opportunities to mirror your group members.

3.2.8 Look for complementary and incongruent messages

As you can see, there are many types of nonverbal communication. Sometimes, a person will simultaneously display two nonverbal messages (or a nonverbal and a verbal message) that support each other. These are called complementary messages. **Complementary messages** are messages that reinforce each other. Think about when someone extends their arm and motions you to sit down while simultaneously smiling and asking you to make yourself comfortable. The extended arm and smile are complementary (nonverbal) messages to the (verbal) message inviting you to make yourself comfortable. Complementary messages help us feel comfortable that our interpretations are accurate.

At other times, people may simultaneously display two nonverbal messages that seem to be at odds with each other. These are considered **incongruent messages**. For example, they may be nodding (suggesting they want to continue the conversation) while they are packing their belongings into their backpack (suggesting they want to end the conversation). Another type of incongruency occurs when someone's nonverbal behavior contradicts their verbal message. For example, someone may welcome you to the group while simultaneously furrowing their brow and crossing their arms across their chest (see Figure 3.2). This incongruence suggests the person may not be sincerely welcoming.

Some amount of incongruency occurs because we are conflicted and have competing desires (such as wanting to continue a conversation and wanting to make it in time to our next meeting). Other incongruencies are more problematic, particularly if they occur often.

When you observe incongruent messages, it is possible the person is being deceptive. In fact, there is a body of literature (both scholarly and popular) that covers "deceptive" behaviors and advises (with varying levels of authority and credibility) us to look out for these nonverbal cues that someone is lying. Although information suggesting that you can be a human lie detector can be entertaining, it is often over-simplified and misguided. There is also research that shows that some "signs" of lying are also signs of neurodiversity or trauma. Just because someone fidgets and doesn't look you in the eye, does not mean they are lying. It might mean that they are extremely uncomfortable with the topic or that they are uncomfortable with direct eye contact.

FIGURE 3.2 Incongruent verbal and nonverbal messages

Rather than trying to spot lies, develop the practice of looking for complementary and incongruent messages to ensure that you are communicating effectively with your team members.

3.3 Remote and technological considerations

Online meetings pose different types of nonverbal challenges for group members. On the one hand, the nonverbal cues are more limited because you typically will only be able to see the face and shoulders of your group members. For this reason, you might not be able to tell, for instance, if a group member is tapping their foot in impatience or fidgeting with their nearby mobile phone in boredom. You might not be able to ascertain if they are exhibiting any incongruent behaviors such as nodding (encouraging you to continue your story) and simultaneously positioning their feet to exit the conversation (indicating you should wrap it up).

On the other hand, research (Bailenson, 2021; Dragomir, Farcas, & Şimon, 2021) on nonverbal communication through video-conferencing tools such as Zoom or Google Meet shows that you have to rely even *more* on both verbal and nonverbal cues. For example, one study showed that participants smiled more "animatedly" and spoke 15% louder when they were on video calls (Croes et al., 2019). Additionally, these technologies may distort the participants' spatial environment, particularly affecting their gaze direction, not knowing when it is their time to speak, leading to a lack of trust among the people involved in the meeting, which is paramount for a good inter-group communication.

(Dragomir, Farcas, & Şimon, 2021, p. 4)

As online meetings are becoming increasingly common, numerous studies point to a common syndrome known as the Zoom Fatigue: "the tiredness, worry, or burnout associated with overusing virtual platforms of communication" (Lee, 2020). Knowing these caveats will help you be more mindful of your own and your audience's nonverbal cues. Although circumstances such as geographical distance or the COVID pandemic may require more virtual meetings and fewer in-person meetings, we should be wary of Zoom Fatigue. When you have the choice, it is very often the best practice to opt for a face-to-face (over online) meeting.

In our facilitation of and participation in both online classes and business meetings, we have observed several nonverbal practices that enhance group collaboration. These include turning on your camera, being mindful of your surroundings and clothing, and monitoring your facial expressions.

3.3.1 Turn on your camera

If you are a student in an online or hybrid course, your instructor should set the expectations for the online class meeting. Some instructors require the cameras to be on; others don't. In some cases (for instance, if participants are hearing-impaired), the instructor may ask that you have your camera off unless you are speaking, so as not to create too many visual distractions. Regardless of the practices for class meetings, individual group meetings benefit from all team members turning their cameras on.

No matter how often we repeat that students in breakout rooms should keep their cameras turned on during group meetings, some students are reluctant to do so. When we, as instructors, enter a Zoom or Microsoft Teams breakout room and hear voices, but do not see any faces or any screen sharing happening, we become concerned. Why? Because without the cameras, our meetings now provide zero nonverbal information to the group members. When you are in an online group meeting, turn on your camera and ask your group members to do the same. Seeing your group members' facial expressions and other gestures provide critical information to you, information that is lost when their cameras are off.

One study (Grayson & Monk, 2003) shows that the webcam should be placed as close to the image of your audience as possible, as your audience can tell when they are being looked at 84% of the time when you place the camera directly above their image. So, try to position your webcam or your eyes so that you are looking straight at the camera when talking to further engage with your audience.

3.3.2 Mind your surroundings and clothing

As you have learned, nonverbal messages include more than facial expressions and body positioning. Nonverbal messages also include the information others gather about you based on your backdrop or surroundings. When the musician Charlie Puth performed online during a charity concert to support frontline workers fighting the COVID pandemic, his backdrop was his bedroom. Just over his shoulder, viewers could clearly see his unmade bed behind him. After the televised One World: Together at Home concert, Twitter was ablaze with comments praising the performance. But there were also tweets pointing out the unmade bed. There were enough comments that Puth responded, "Ooops I forgot to make my bed" (Puth, 2020).

As a musician, Puth likely enjoyed the comments extolling the strength of his performance. Our guess is that he enjoyed the unmade bed comments much less. Did the unmade bed have any bearing on the performance? Perhaps not directly, but the point here is this: Did Puth want his audience to associate him with his failings as a housekeeper, or would he have preferred they focused their evaluations on his musical performance? In the same manner, your surroundings can influence the perception your team members have about you. Do you want your team members to associate you with your failings as a housekeeper or do you want them to associate you with your strong contributions to the team?

Your surroundings can be distracting and can send messages you don't intend to convey. To mitigate this risk, be mindful of what can be seen behind and around you when you are on camera. Be aware that you might need to change something about your surroundings or change your location.

In a survey conducted by the *Harvard Business Review* (Zandan & Lynch, 2020), where over 450 male and female respondents were asked about their video conferencing preferences, 60% showed a clear preference for the background behind you: Most of them prefer seeing the room behind you and very few prefer the fake virtual/ scenic backgrounds. Only 39% of respondents claimed a clear preference for clothing color worn by the speaker (neutral colors), but nearly half prefer seeing business casual attire. Therefore, check your video preview before joining a meeting and consider using the "blur background" function in these online meeting platforms to ensure that you are conveying the messages you intend to convey.

3.3.3 Monitor your facial expressions

Depending on the size of your group, the online environment may provide a larger, clearer picture of your team members' facial expressions than if you were sitting across the table from them. The impact of nonverbal communication such as facial expressions and eye contact may also be heightened in online meetings because we do not have other nonverbal cues (such as position of arms or feet) that are observable in face-to-face meetings. For these reasons, it is helpful to monitor your facial expressions online.

In online meetings, we have seen team members who are actively grimacing or yawning. As we know, facial expressions such as these could trigger corresponding feelings in your group members. One study (Rößler, Sun, & Gloor, 2021) found that there is a positive correlation between the speaker's mood and the audience's mood. These researchers recommend that presenters convey enthusiasm and positive energy to the audience, because their results show that the happier the speaker is, the happier the audience is. We have found this same connection within groups. Group members often tend to be more open to someone who presents their ideas in an enthusiastic manner.

If you are uncertain about how you might be presenting yourself in an online meeting, check your own image and monitor your own nonverbal messages. Depending on the platform you use and the setting you select, there are ways to see yourself in an online meeting. For instance, with some settings, you can see yourself in a type of picture within a picture. We recommend that you take advantage of this feature by occasionally checking your own body position and facial expressions.

3.4 Summary

This chapter explains the following key points about nonverbal communication for group collaboration:

- In a group meeting, position your chair and body so that you have an open line of sight to all group members.
- Communicate interest in and engagement with the speaker by looking them in the eye when they are talking.
- Unless smiling is seen as disrespectful (or otherwise negatively) by the culture in which you are working, choose a pleasant smile over a neutral expression to greet your group members.
- To boost your own self-confidence and your group members' confidence in what you're saying, nod while speaking. However, nods don't always mean agreement; sometimes they mean someone is "tracking" with you.
- To be perceived as more credible, use hand gestures to emphasize your points.
- In your group conversations, look for opportunities to mirror others to show agreement.
- Look for complementary and incongruent nonverbal behaviors.
- In online meetings, turn on your camera, mind your surroundings and clothing, and monitor facial expressions.

3.5 Discussion questions

1. Besides what is mentioned in this chapter, what additional nonverbal cues have you seen in groups (and what might they indicate)?

2.   What types of haptic communication have you seen in the teams in which you are involved?
3.   Besides creating a round table, what are some additional ways you could position your in-person group to allow for more interaction?
4.   What troubling or annoying nonverbal behaviors have you seen in online group meetings?

3.6 Activities

3.6.1 Synchronized claps

This in-person activity proves that eye contact is not as easy as it looks! This game forces students to pay attention and to look other players in the eye. Synchronizing precise, nonverbal communication to coordinate actions helps students with interaction, starting small.

Object: The object of this game is to clap at the exact same time as the person to whom you are "passing" the clap. The only way to successfully achieve this is to make direct eye contact with that person, so that you can synchronize your clap.

Setup: Group stands in a circle.

Activity:

1.   One person volunteers to start. That person makes eye contact with a person to their left, and both try to clap simultaneously. If they do not clap at the same time, they must repeat until they are synchronized.
2.   The person who successfully "receives" the clap then continues to pass the clap to the person on their left, and so on.
3.   Once the clap has made it around the group, players have the option of "reversing" the clap, that is, giving it back to the person who just gave it to them.
4.   In the third round, people can make eye contact with anyone in the circle and pass the clap to that person, who then selects someone else in the group to whom to pass the clap. Any time players are not synchronized in their clap, they must redo it until they clap at the same time.

Take-away: To coordinate your movements with another, it is important to sustain eye contact. Eye contact is also important in many group contexts, including when you are listening and expressing empathy.

3.6.2 The mirror game

This activity, which can be done either online or in-person, provides group members experience in making eye contact and actively synchronizing their movements. The activity allows participants to feel what it is like to be in sync with someone else.

Object: To have pairs of team members perfectly synchronize their movements so that an onlooker cannot determine which person is following and which is leading.

Setup: In an in-person environment, have partners stand a few feet apart and face each other. In an online environment, put group members in pairs, send each pair to a breakout room, and have them turn on their cameras and stand in front of the camera so that they have an unobscured view of their partner.

Activity: There should be no talking for the duration of this activity. One person in each pair will be the leader. This person will lead three synchronized breaths (breath in and out, slowly, together). Next, the leader will slowly start to move parts of their body (including their face), and the follower will mimic the actions real-time. For instance, the leader may slowly raise their eyebrows then raise both hands above the head, then turn their head to the left. The follower will simultaneously mirror all of these actions. The leader should be continuously moving and building up to a faster pace. The goal is for the two to move in a completely synchronized manner.

Take-away: When you coordinate your movements with another, you experience what it is like to be in-synch with them. Aim for a similar sort of in-synch feeling when you are working with them.

References

Abele, A., & Yzerbyt, V. (2021). Body posture and interpersonal perception in a dyadic interaction: A Big Two analysis. *European Journal of Social Psychology*, 51(1), 23–39. https://doi.org/10.1002/ejsp.2711.

Ashton-James, C. E., & Chartrand, T. L. (2009). Social cues for creativity: The impact of behavioral mimicry on convergent and divergent thinking. *Journal of Experimental Social Psychology*, 45(4), 1036–1040. https://doi.org/10.1016/j.jesp.2009.03.030.

Bailenson, J. N. (2021). Nonverbal overload: A theoretical argument for the causes of Zoom Fatigue. *Technology, Mind, and Behavior*, 2(1), 1–6.

Barnett, G. (2015). *Play the part: Master signals to connect and communicate for business success.* McGraw Hill Education.

Bornschein, A. (2013). Heirs of the round table: French Arthurian fiction from 1977 to the present. [Doctoral dissertation, University of Pennsylvania]. Publicly Accessible Penn Dissertations. 836. https://repository.upenn.edu/edissertations/836.

Briñol, P., & Petty, R. E. (2003). Overt head movements and persuasion: A self-validation analysis. *Journal of Personality and Social Psychology*, 84(6), 1123–1139. https://doi.org/10.1037/0022-3513.83.6.1123.

Brooks, D. C. (2012). Space and consequences: The impact of different formal learning spaces on instructor and student behavior. *Journal of Learning Spaces*, 1(2).

Casasanto, D., & Jasmin, K. (2010). Good and bad in the hands of politicians: Spontaneous gestures during positive and negative speech. *PloS One*, 5(7), e11805–e11805. https://doi.org/10.1371/journal.pone.0011805.

Chaplin, W. F., Phillips, J. B., Brown, J. D., Clanton, N. R., & Stein, J. L. (2000). Handshaking, gender, personality and first impressions. *Journal of Personality and Social Psychology*, 79, 110–117.

Clough, S., & Duff, M. C. (2020). The role of gesture in communication and cognition: Implications for understanding and treating neurogenic communication disorders. *Frontiers in Human Neuroscience*, 14, 323–323. https://doi.org/10.3389/fnhum.2020.00323.

Croes, E. A. J., Antheunis, M. L., Schouten, A. P., & Krahmer, E. J. (2019). Social attraction in video-mediated communication: The role of nonverbal affiliative behavior. *Journal of Social and Personal Relationships*, 36(4), 1210–1232. https://doi.org/10.1177/0265407518757382.

Devito, J. A. (2019). *The interpersonal communication book*. Pearson.

Dragomir, G., Farcas, M. A. & Şimon, S. (2021). Students' perceptions of verbal and non-verbal communication behaviors during and after the COVID-19 pandemic. *Applied Sciences*, 11(18), 8282. https://doi.org/10.3390/app11188282.

Elle. (2020). 37 notorious non-smiling celebrities, smilinG. *Elle*, February 20. www.elle.com/culture/celebrities/g9371/celebrities-who-do-not-smile-smiling/.

Fernandes, A. C., Huang, J., & Rinaldo, V. (2011). Does where a student sits really matter?–the impact of seating locations on student classroom learning. *International Journal of Applied Educational Studies*, 10(1), 66–77.

Goldin-Meadow, S., & Alibali, M. W. (2013). Gesture's role in speaking, learning, and creating language. *Annual Review of Psychology*, 64(1), 257–283. https://doi.org/10.1146/annurev-psych-113011-143802.

Grayson, D. & Monk, A. (2003). Are you looking at me? Eye contact and desktop video conferencing. *ACM Transactions on Computer-Human Interaction*, 10(3), 221–243. https://doi.org/10.1145/937549.937552.

Körner, R., Petersen, L.-E., & Schütz, A. (2019). Do expansive or contractive body postures affect feelings of self-worth? High power poses impact state self-esteem. *Current Psychology*, 40(8), 4112–4123. https://doi.org/10.1007/s12144-019-00371-1.

Kraus, M. W., Huang, C., & Keltner, D. (2010). Tactile communication, cooperation, and performance: An ethological study of the NBA. *Emotion*, 10(5), 745–749. https://doi.org/10.1037/a0019382.

Krumhuber, E., Manstead, A. S. R., Cosker, D., Marshall, D., & Rosin, P. L. (2008). Effects of dynamic attributes of smiles in human and synthetic faces: A simulated job interview setting. *Journal of Nonverbal Behavior*, 33(1), 1–15. https://doi.org/10.1007/s10919-008-0056-8.

Krys, K., Vauclair, M., Capaldi, C. A., Lun, V. M.-C., Bond, M. H., Domínguez-Espinosa, A., Torres, C., Lipp, O. V., Manickam, L. S. S., Xing, C., Antalíková, R., Pavlopoulos, V., Teyssier, J., Hur, T., Hansen, K., Szarota, P., Ahmed, R. A., Burtceva, E., Chkhaidze, A.,...Yu, A. A. (2015). Be careful where you smile: Culture shapes judgments of intelligence and honesty of smiling individuals. *Journal of Nonverbal Behavior*, 40(2), 101–116. https://doi.org/10.1007/s10919-015-0226-4.

Lee, J. (2020). A neuropsychological exploration of Zoom fatigue. *The Psychiatric Times*, 37 (11), 38.

Matschke, X., & Rieger, M. C. (2021). Kisses, handshakes, COVID-19–Will the pandemic change us forever? *Review of Behavioral Economics*, 8(1), 25–46. http://dx.doi.org/10.1561/105.00000132.

Mehrabian, A. (1981). *Silent messages: Implicit communication of emotions and attitudes*. Wadsworth Pub. Co.

Meza-de-Luna, M., Terven, J. R., Raducanu, B., & Salas, J. (2018). Assessing the influence of mirroring on the perception of professional competence using wearable technology. *IEEE Transactions on Affective Computing*, 9(2), 161–175. https://doi.org/10.1109/TAFFC.2016.2606594.

Nagy, E., Farkas, T., Guy, F., & Stafylarakis, A. (2020). Effects of handshake duration on other nonverbal behavior. *Perceptual and Motor Skills*, 127(1), 52–73. https://doi.org/10.1177/0031512519876743.

Partala, T., & Surakka, V. (2003). Pupil size variation as an indication of affective processing. *International Journal of Human-Computer Studies*, 59(1), 185–198. https://doi.org/10.1016/S1071-5819(03)00017-X99

Pi, Z., Zhu, F., Zhang, Y., Chen, L., & Yang, J. (2022). Complexity of visual learning material moderates the effects of instructor's beat gestures and head nods in video lectures. *Learning and Instruction*, 77, 101520. https://doi.org/10.1016/j.learninstruc.2021.101520.

Puth, C. (2020). Ooops I forgot to make my bed. @CharliePuth, Twitter, April 18. https://twitter.com/charlieputh/status/1251621533228752896?ref_src=twsrc%5Etfw.

Rößler, J., Sun, J., & Gloor, P. (2021). Reducing videoconferencing fatigue through facial emotion recognition. *Future Internet*, 13(5), 126. https://doi.org/10.3390/fi13050126.

Saunders, R. A., Klawohn, J., & Inzlicht, M. (2018). Interpersonal touch enhances cognitive control: A neurophysiological investigation. *Journal of Experimental Psychology. General*, 147(7), 1066–1077. https://doi.org/10.1037/xge0000412.

Vicario, C. M., & Newman, A. (2013). Emotions affect the recognition of hand gestures. *Frontiers in Human Neuroscience*, 7, 906–906. https://doi.org/10.3389/fnhum.2013.00906.

Zandan, N. & Lynch, H. (2020). Dress for the (remote) job you want. *Harvard Business Review*, June 18. https://hbr.org/2020/06/dress-for-the-remote-job-you-want.

4

PRACTICING EMPATHY

Questions to consider

- What is the difference between sympathy and empathy?
- Why is it important to be inquisitive about others' opinions?
- What happens in your brain when you observe people?
- How can you practice active inquiry?
- What are the benefits of self-disclosure?
- How can you be more considerate?

4.1 Introduction

Empathy is an essential building block of collaboration. But, a lot of people are fuzzy on empathy or confuse it with sympathy. You may have learned that "empathy is walking a mile in someone's shoes." But what does that mean, and how does it differ from sympathy?

Sympathy is having the same perspective or experience as someone else. For instance, if your cat has died, you can sympathize with someone whose cat has died. But if you love all dogs, and you meet someone who is afraid of dogs, you can't sympathize with them. You do not share their perspective or experiences. Instead, you can attempt to empathize with them. **Empathy** is appreciating a perspective or experience that you do not share.

In our experience, empathy is one of the most critical aspects of group collaboration. Unfortunately, it is often ignored.

DOI: 10.4324/9781003285571-5

4.2 Empathy practices

While some people are naturally empathetic—empathy is a skill that can be built. We have found that the following practices can hone your empathy skills.

4.2.1 Appreciate that everyone has a unique perspective

Do you think that all rational people use the same approach to decision making? If you were to design a product, would you assume that any sensible user could intuitively figure out how to use it? It might be a surprise to you, but people (even other rational people) do not all arrive at decisions the way you do. However, children, teens, and some adults have a tendency to have an egocentric view of the world. Being able to appreciate an issue from another person's perspective is something that typically develops over time. In fact, research (Arain et al., 2013) shows that the human brain continues to mature until the early twenties. It is a mistake to assume that all reasonable people share one perspective. This is the reason it makes sense to be inquisitive about others' perspectives.

Each of us has a unique combination of experiences, observations, and contexts that contribute to our worldview or perspective. It is ridiculous to assume that everyone thinks like we do, and for successful collaboration we need to understand this point. Once we appreciate that such differences exist, we are in a better position to try to understand a perspective other than our own. As Seelig (2012) explains, empathy involves changing your frame of reference, shifting your perspective, and looking at a problem from the other's point of view.

Don't assume that everyone thinks like you.

4.2.2 Observe people

Have you ever watched a mother feeding her baby a jar of food? The mother's mouth will mimic the opening and closing of the baby's mouth. Research in neuropsychology suggests that this behavior is the result of mirror neurons, which fire both when a person acts (in the case, the baby eating) and when another person (in this case, the mother) observes this action. In other words, the mother's neurons "mirror" the behavior of the baby, as though the mother were herself eating. Similarly, experiments (e.g., Botvinick et al., 2005; Cheng et al., 2008; Morrison et al. 2004; Lamm et al. 2007) have shown that certain regions of the brain (the anterior insula, anterior cingulate cortex, and inferior frontal cortex) are active both when people experience an emotion directly and when they see another person experiencing that emotion.

While there is no conclusive evidence about the role of mirror neurons in human empathy, some neuroscientists have argued that mirror neuron systems in the human brain help us understand the actions and intentions of others. One study (Botvinick et al., 2005) found that individuals viewing facial expressions of pain were found to engage areas of the brain (anterior cingulate cortex and insula) that are also engaged by the first-hand experience of pain. Other researchers (Iacoboni et al., 2005) describe how the premotor mirror neuron areas, which are active during the execution and the observation of an action by someone else, are also involved in understanding the intentions of others.

Mirror neurons aside, observation is a powerful interpersonal skill. Observation provides you with information. If you notice a member of your group is frowning and has a clenched jaw, you have some indication of their state of mind or temperament. If another group member is continuously yawning throughout your presentation, you might have information about how much (or little) they are enjoying your presentation. Observing people will not only give you insight into them, but it can also validate (or invalidate) your assumptions about them. For instance, if Carolyn was yawning throughout your presentation, and she was also yawning through lunch, this could invalidate your belief that Carolyn found your presentation boring. She might simply be tired.

User experience (UX) designers often observe potential users working with early prototypes of products so they (the UX designers) can see how the users actually interact with the product and what tasks are easy or difficult to manage. When you observe others at their jobs, in their homes, in new situations, you learn about them. Watching their actions, interactions, and nonverbal behaviors gives you a plethora of information.

Observing the behaviors and nonverbal communication of others can provide insight into who they are.

4.2.3 Be curious about people

Have you ever had an intriguing conversation with someone you didn't know? If you are truly interested in other people, you might have these types of conversations frequently. In his book, *Empathy*, Roman Krznaric (2015) explains that the single trait that all empathetic people share is their "insatiable curiosity about other human beings" (p. 99). Krznaric emphasizes the importance of conversation and treating conversation as a craft, as opposed to a technique. Techniques or tools, he explains, can make conversations stilted and artificial.

Being authentically curious about people and the ways they think is a great way to express empathy on a team. Your questions allow your teammates to explain themselves and allow you to discover new information and to better understand the perspective of your teammates. Figure 4.1 shows an example of being authentically curious about a teammate. Approaching your team members and the work of the team with curiosity also primes you to consider alternatives to the ways you typically approach tasks or challenges. This curiosity often leads to new ways of solving problems.

In addition, research shows that curious people are found to possess multiple adaptive behaviors including a tolerance of uncertainty, a non-defensive attitude

FIGURE 4.1 Example of authentic curiosity

(Kashdan et al., 2013), improved psychological well-being, and a decrease in emotional exhaustion (Wang & Li, 2015, p. 138). These same behaviors allow you to be even more empathetic.

No interpersonal tips or techniques will yield as much success as possessing a sincere curiosity about others.

4.2.4 Practice active inquiry

In conversations, do you ask questions? What types of questions do you ask? Questions are a critical part of conversation. But not all questions are equal. Active inquiry is not about learning objective "facts." It is about engaging in a process whereby you come to be able to articulate or appreciate another's perspective, opinion, or belief. Asking questions about someone's ideas lets them know that you are curious about or interested in them. This is a skill that children are generally good at, but some adults stop practicing.

As we discuss in Chapter 1, questions are an essential element in conversation. Not only are questions a good way to make conversation with your group members, but questions also allow you to express empathy. You don't have to be an "extrovert" to be able to ask people questions. In fact, people who are skilled listeners often put others at ease because they don't overwhelm others with their "force of character" (Krznaric, 2015, p. 104).

For example, when you are discussing job candidates for a position in your company, you can practice active inquiry by asking the interviewing team simple, open-ended questions, like, "What do you like best about candidate A?" Then, after your teammate responds, ask follow-up and clarifying questions. If your teammate responds that candidate A has five years of programming experience, you might follow-up with, "Is programming experience the primary qualification we are looking for? Are there other important qualifications we need to consider?"

If you are not accustomed to asking follow-up questions, you might be afraid that you sound like you are interrogating someone. Rather than thinking of follow-up questions in this way, consider them an organic part of an informal interview. In an interview, follow-up questions are naturally arising and help you probe for additional details while exploring the ideas and statements of your teammates. An added bonus to asking follow-up questions is that research (Huang et al., 2017) shows that people who probe for information not only learn more accurate information about others, but they are also better liked!

Look for opportunities to "interview" others. This will help you build an appreciation for other perspectives.

4.2.5 Practice self-disclosure

How much do other people share with you about themselves? How open are you with others? Is there a correlation between the two? When we disclose personal information about ourselves, it encourages others to do the same.

Self-disclosure is something that people tend to do more in one-on-one conversations than in group settings. However, the information being disclosed generally dictates to whom it is disclosed. If I have a problem remembering names or if I am nervous about public speaking, I might be comfortable disclosing this with my entire team, or I might only share this with 1–2 group members I believe would be sympathetic or empathetic.

Self-disclosure has a few benefits. First, it allows us to connect with another person. Second, it allows us to show that we are human. But self-disclosure also makes us vulnerable. Because of this, many people only disclose information about themselves if they trust another person. Trust and self-disclosure have a reciprocal relationship. Since disclosing personal information makes a person vulnerable, it also opens up the door to build relationships.

Research (e.g., Collins & Miller, 1994; Reis & Shaver, 1988) has long shown that disclosing information about ourselves strengthens our relationships with others. The connection between self-disclosure, vulnerability, and trust building is further confirmed by teamwork researcher Daniel Coyle (2018). Citing vulnerability researcher Harvard professor Jeff Polzer, Coyle argues that showing vulnerability can help build a stronger team. This is because when you show your vulnerability, the other person responds by signaling their own vulnerability, and this continuous loop helps build closeness and trust.

To allow your teammate to learn more about you and your ideas, you can disclose (relevant and appropriate) personal information about yourself. If practicing self-disclosure does not seem natural to you, allow your team members to take the lead. If a teammate confides some mistake they made or a shortcoming they have, they are trusting you with personal information. If this happens, you might consider sharing something equally as personal with them at some point in the future.

Sometimes, you may not be comfortable casually sharing personal information with people. Self-disclosure may not be your style. This is when more "formalized" activities can be used in your groups to effect mutual self-disclosure. Lorelie Parolin, US learning lead and dean of Hamburger University for McDonald's Corporation describes a journey map activity she uses with some of her teams to help build a supportive environment. She has each team member draw a line that represents their life from birth through today. Above that line, she has them Map 3–4 moments in their personal life that were particularly exciting or energizing for them. Below the line, she asks for 3–4 moments when they felt particularly demotivated or upset. When team members share their journey maps with each other, she asks, "Why was this moment a high or why was it a low?" As Parolin explains, "Through this activity, you can learn a lot about what motivates and demotivates group members. You can then use this knowledge to keep each other motivated throughout the project." See Activity 4.6.2 to practice this activity.

To learn about others, share information about yourself.

4.2.6 Be considerate

When you have empathy for your team members, you are more likely to be considerate of them. Think of empathy as trying to understand another person's perspective and being considerate as taking action based on that understanding.

For instance, if you are going to miss a deadline, inform your teammates as early as you can. Sometimes people think their team won't notice if they missed a deadline, or they are embarrassed to admit that they did not meet the deadline. However, when you are working on a team, very often your teammates' work will be contingent on yours (and vice versa). Missing a deadline is not ideal but missing a deadline and leaving your team in the dark about missing it is worse. As soon as you realize that you will not be able to meet a deadline, let your group know and work with them to make any necessary adjustments to the project plan. For more information about project plans, see Chapter 9.

Another way to be considerate to your teammates is to attempt to be on time for your meetings or to even arrive a bit early. If you cannot avoid being late, let your teammates know. A simple text or phone call letting them know that you will be late and the time you expect to arrive will help the group make any adjustments they need. It will also let your team members know that you respect them and value their time. As soon as you detect an issue that may cause you to be late, contact one or more of your teammates to let them know.

Empathetic teammates are considerate of each other.

4.3 Remote and technological considerations

Virtual environments can be tough to navigate, and expressing empathy online is especially challenging. While a physical setting allows you to make direct eye contact with individual team members or give them a supportive nod, the virtual setting only allows you to make eye contact with the camera. The limitations of virtual technology make it both difficult and important to make a conscious effort to express empathy.

As we discuss in Chapter 3, many nonverbal cues that we rely on during in-person communication are absent online. When expressing empathy online, it may be necessary for you to name an individual. For instance, you might state, "Jeremy, it sounds like you've got a crazy schedule today," or ask, "Rasheed, what can we do to help you meet this deadline?" At first, such direct conversation may feel overly formal or awkward, but it compensates for the limitations of online media.

Another way to compensate for the limitations of online meetings is to use the chat feature. Some platforms allow you to send private messages to one or more individuals without derailing the conversation at hand. If a teammate expressed an unpopular opinion in a meeting and you want to tell her that she handled it well, you can send a private message or even a text.

Even in online settings, you can practice the skills that we present in this chapter (observing people, being curious, and practicing active inquiry). This is one reason we ask people to turn on their cameras in video calls.

Virtual conversations can allow you to empathetically connect with others, but they may take more time and effort.

4.4 Summary

This chapter explains the following key points about developing and practicing empathy:

- Be appreciative of others' perspectives.
- Observe the behaviors and nonverbal communication of your group members.
- Be sincerely curious about others.
- Practice active inquiry by looking for opportunities to informally interview others.

- Ask your teammates questions and share information about yourself.
- Treat your teammates considerately.

4.5 Discussion questions

1. When was the last time you empathized with someone?
2. What is one aspect of your life that you wish others would empathize with?
3. When you meet a new person, what kind of information about yourself do you tend to disclose first?
4. What about others do you find yourself most curious about (e.g., what is their taste in music or fashion, or if they are a dog or cat person)?

4.6 Activities

4.6.1 Sharing moodboards

This activity can be done in either an online or an in-person setting. It incorporates several of the empathy-honing practices explained in this chapter, namely, practicing self-disclosure, being curious about people, practicing active inquiry, and listening to people.

Object: The object of this activity is to learn more about your group members and any connections you might have.

Prework: Before the activity, individuals should compose a personal moodboard, which is simply a collage of images and words with which they identify and would be comfortable sharing. Have individuals use a Microsoft Word document or direct them to a free, simple template (e.g., GoMoodBoard.com) to compile an eight to ten image collage.

Activity:

1. If you are doing this activity in person and you have more than four group members, subdivide your groups and give them space to work. *If you are meeting online, be sure to assign individuals to particular breakout rooms (e.g., Zoom) or channels (e.g., MS Teams) for the activity.*
2. During the activity, the first individuals should share their moodboard, providing any explanation they want.
3. After the first group member has shared their moodboard, the other group members should answer the following questions (aloud) for the group:

   a   Which image most surprised you and why?
   b   Which image(s) did you identify with?

4. After all groups have shared and returned to the main group, start the discussion by explaining that when you expose information about yourself, you are bound

to learn about others. Asking pertinent questions and listening effectively can help you begin to understand others. When people feel understood, they are typically more willing collaborators. *If you are working online, close breakout rooms and/or have students return to the main room before the debrief.*

Post-activity discussion questions:

1. What types of surprises did you encounter when you viewed your team-mate's moodboards?
2. What commonalities did you find with other group members?
3. With what groups and in what situations could you use this moodboard activity?

Take-away: Sharing can be sparked by visual images.

4.6.2 Journey mapping

This activity can be used in either an in-person or online setting. It allows us to appreciate what motivates and demotivates members of your team.

Object: The object of this activity is to practice self-disclosure and to help build a supportive environment for your team.

Setup: To prepare for this activity, each person should have a sheet of paper and a pencil or pen.

Activity:

Part I (Individually).

1. Turn the blank page so that it is in landscape view and draw a line that extends from the left to the right side of the paper.
2. Mark the start of the line with "birth" and the end with "today."
3. Above that line, map 3–4 moments in your personal life that were particularly exciting or energizing for you.
4. Below the line, map 2–3 moments when you felt particularly demoti-vated or upset.

Part II (With the group).

1. The first person should present their map and explain why each moment was a "high" or a "low."
2. The other group members should look for common themes in the explanations that the presenter has provided and share these with the presenter.
3. Repeat 1–2 until all group members have shared.

Post-activity discussion questions:

1. What types of themes did the group identify with "high moments?" (These are the motivators.)
2. What types of themes did the group identify with "low moments?" (These are the demotivators.)
3. Are the same motivators and demotivators in place for you in the workplace? How are they similar or different?
4. What have you learned about your teammates through this activity?

Take-away: Very often, the things that motivate (or demotivate) us in our personal lives also motivate us in our professional lives. Understanding what motivates and demotivates our team members helps us to better understand them and express empathy for them.

References

Arain, M., Haque, M., Johal, L., Mathur, P., Nel, W., Rais, A., Sandhu, R., & Sharma, S. (2013). Maturation of the adolescent brain. *Neuropsychiatric Disease and Treatment*, 9, 449–461. https://doi.org/10.2147/NDT.S39776.

Atkinson, J. K., & Hewitt, O. (2019). Do group interventions help people with autism spectrum disorder to develop better relationships with others? A critical review of the literature. *British Journal of Learning Disabilities*, 47(2), 77–90. https://doi.org/10.1111/bld.12258.

Botvinick, M., Jha, A. P., Bylsma, L. M., Fabian, S. A., Solomon, P. E., & Prkachin, K. M. (2005). Viewing facial expressions of pain engages cortical areas involved in the direct experience of pain. *NeuroImage*, 25(1): 312–319. https://doi.org/10.1016/j.neuroimage.2004.11.043.

Cheng, Y., Yang, C. Y., Lin, C. P., Lee, P. L., Decety, J. (2008). The perception of pain in others suppresses somatosensory oscillations: a magnetoencephalography study. *NeuroImage*, 40(4): 1833–1840. https://doi.org/10.1016/j.neuroimage.2008.01.064.

Collins, N. L., & Miller, L. C. (1994). Self-disclosure and liking: A meta-analytic review. *Psychological Bulletin*, 116, 457–475. https://doi.org/10.1037/0033-2909.116.3.457.

Coyle, D. (2018). *The culture code: The secrets of highly successful groups*. Bantam Books.

Huang, K., Yeomans, M., Brooks, A. W., Minson, J., & Gino, F. (2017). It doesn't hurt to ask: Question-asking increases liking. *Journal of Personality and Social Psychology*, 113(3), 430–452. https://doi.org/10.1037/pspi0000097.

Iacoboni, M., Molnar-Szakacs, I, Gallese, V., Buccino, G., & Mazziotta, J. C. (2005) Grasping the intentions of others with one's own mirror neuron system. *PLoS Biol* 3(3), e79.

Kashdan, T. B., Sherman, R. A., Yarbro, J., & Funder, D. C. (2013). How are curious people viewed and how do they behave in social situations? From the perspectives of self, friends, parents, and unacquainted observers. *Journal of Personality*, 81(2), 142–154. https://doi.org/10.1111/j.1467-6494.2012.00796.x.

Krznaric, R. (2015). *Empathy*. Perigee.

Lamm, C., Batson, C. D., & Decety, J. (2007). The neural substrate of human empathy: Effects of perspective-taking and cognitive appraisal. *Journal of Cognitive Neuroscience*, 19(1): 42–58. https://doi.org/10.1162/jocn.2007.19.1.42.

Morrison, I., Lloyd, D., Di Pellegrino, G., & Roberts, N. (2004). Vicarious responses to pain in anterior cingulate cortex: Is empathy a multisensory issue? *Cognitive, Affective, & Behavioral Neuroscience*, 4(2): 270–278. https://doi.org/10.3758/CABN.4.2.270.

Parker, T. (1996). *Studs Terkel: A life in words*. Henry Holt.

Reis, H. T., & Shaver, P. (1988). Intimacy as an interpersonal process. In S. Duck (Ed.), *Handbook of personal relationships* (pp. 367–389). Wiley.

Seelig, T. (2012). *inGenius: A crash course on creativity*. HarperCollins.

Wang, H., & Li, J. (2015). How trait curiosity influences psychological well-being and emotional exhaustion: The mediating role of personal initiative. *Personality and Individual Differences*, 75, 135–140. https://doi.org/10.1016/j.paid.2014.11.020.

5

SHARING IDEAS

Questions to consider

- What is one method for summarizing your ideas?
- How can a rule of improvisation inform the way we present our ideas?
- How can you gain confidence in presenting your ideas?
- How do group members typically respond to bragging?
- How can you guard against ideas being lost?
- What method can you use to capture diverse ideas?

5.1 Introduction to sharing ideas

So far, we have covered several interpersonal skills that are important to effective group collaboration. These skills involve listening, being mindful of nonverbal messages, and exhibiting empathy. You will be using these skills while interacting with your group members and completing the work with which your group is tasked. However, the nature of strong groups is such that there will often be different ideas about how to accomplish the work of the group. For this reason, each group member must be prepared both to share their own ideas and to consider the ideas of others in the group. Not everyone is equally comfortable or adept at presenting their ideas to a group, so this chapter provides some tactics for sharing your ideas. This chapter also presents techniques for considering the ideas of others.

5.2 Practices for sharing ideas

The following practices will help you share your ideas and explore the ideas of others in your group.

DOI: 10.4324/9781003285571-6

5.2.1 Summarize your ideas

We find that many students struggle with summarizing their work or ideas at varying levels of technicality (for different audiences). Typically, this struggle encompasses not being able to provide an overview of their work and includes difficulties in both written and presentation forms. We see the same types of deficits in some working professionals who cannot draft executive summaries for supervisors or instructions for non-technical people.

To address this challenge, we teach students and business professionals alike the value of creating and committing to memory a "30-second elevator speech," which is a compact description of their project work that they can recite in the event that someone wants an update. This elevator speech idea is similar to the Pecha-Kucha presentation style (which we recommend in Chapter 6), which imposes time constraints to force the presenter to be concise and the presentation to be visually oriented. Students and working professionals in various disciplines, ranging from nursing to business, are introduced to elevator speeches in their schooling, and we encourage groups to have similar speeches "ready to go" for those spontaneous opportunities where they have very little time to promote their ideas (within the group) and to explain the group's work (outside of the group).

Another idea for summarizing ideas comes from Paul Hellman. In his book, *You've Got 8 Seconds: Communication Secrets for a Distracted World*, Hellman explains that if you have a message to share, start with the conclusion (Hellman, 2017). Next, show your audience how you arrived at that conclusion, and finally, restate the conclusion. For instance, if you want your team to choose one mobile format over another, first state the conclusion ("I propose we select format A"). Next, show them how you arrived at that conclusion ("Format A adheres to principles of visual design, yet still has an Edwardian flair"). Finally, repeat your conclusion ("We should select Format A").

Practice editing your ideas for conciseness. Then, edit the edits to be more concise.

5.2.2 Link ideas

An effective way to share an idea with your team is to link it to something that has previously been offered. Of course, this practice requires that you have been listening to the ideas of your group members! If you are listening to your teammates, it will be easier to connect your ideas to theirs. The importance of listening to your team members is further explained in Chapter 2. In fact, some of the most novel ideas to emerge from groups are combinations that arise when a group member adopts the "yes, and …" rule of improvisation (which is explained in the Introduction to this text). Linking ideas means that you give credit to a previous idea (presented by another group member) and then refine it to include something additional.

For instance, if Indra suggested that the answer to low employee morale is to offer a telecommuting option, you might state, "Indra's idea about the telecommuting option could work, especially if we assure management that we will continue to run our weekly productivity reports." Figure 5.1 shows how you could link to a previous idea.

Linking ideas also means that your group is not continually restarting at the ideation phase. **Ideation** is a term that is used in several fields, including design and usability and refers to the formation of ideas. By linking your idea to another idea, you can move the project forward. Moving forward might mean that you continue to refine your ideas, or to develop a prototype, or perhaps even move on to a new part of the project.

We regularly coach our students to build on the ideas of others. Instead of only offering new ideas, we suggest giving credit to earlier ideas and then building on them.

5.2.3 Challenge yourself to step back

Recently, a student in one of our classes noted that she gets completely stressed out when she has to work in a group. It turns out that this student's typical behavior in previous groups was to jump in and take responsibility for the majority of the group tasks. She explained that she did this because she worried

FIGURE 5.1 Example of linking ideas

that no one else in the group would step up, and the project would fail. To stave off the anxiety this fear produced, the student put a lot of pressure on herself to take control and make sure things got done, which led her to experience even more anxiety.

Once this student was aware of her tendency, she purposely tried to change this attitude and her related group behaviors. Instead of immediately jumping in, she stepped back and trusted that her group members would produce. The act of stepping back made her relax because she was not overly concerned with the minutia of how group members completed their tasks. The student then described how she felt less stressed because she recognized that she, alone, was not in charge of the outcome. As she explained, "It was cathartic for me to give up control and step back. I still diffused tension if something came up but it was nice to not care too much about the way that things got done."

If you are the type of team member who always takes the lead, it is likely that you have also suffered from the type of anxiety this student experienced. Consider taking a step back and putting faith in your group members.

5.2.4 Be assertive and confident

Your group may have some members who, for a variety of reasons, do not fully engage with the team. But it is important that all group members present their ideas assertively and with confidence. Authors of *Group Dynamics for Teams*, Levi and Askay (2021), explain that assertiveness "equalizes power among team members" (p. 168). An assertive team member believes that what they are saying is important, and they do not allow themself to be bulldozed by other group members. **Bulldozing** happens when a team member's ideas are undermined or ignored (effectively flattened) by another team member who may be more dominating, self-assured, or vocal.

One behavior we have noticed with less confident group members is their tendency to present an idea and then immediately back down and provide reasons the group probably shouldn't consider their idea. Group members who do this are effectively sabotaging themselves. A better tactic than shooting down your own idea is to present the idea and then be quiet, allowing the group time to consider it. Once you've shared an idea, try to remain comfortable with the silence that may follow. As Biali Haas (2019) explains, filling in the silence with self-deprecation, apologies, or alternatives will only reveal your insecurity. If you have a hard time refraining from such actions, she recommends making your statement and then "counting back from ten or twenty in your head, while you allow the silence to sit there."

One way to gain confidence is to be sure to review the agenda and any other relevant meeting materials before the meeting. Note areas where you might have comments or questions. You can further build your confidence by researching and gathering data that will support your ideas. Once you have this backup, you will feel less like you are putting *yourself* out there but are putting *your idea* (supported with data) out there. Of course, it is important to differentiate assertiveness from aggressiveness. Where assertiveness focuses on clear and confident communication, aggressiveness is characterized by force, criticism, and negativity (Levi & Askay, 2021). Steer clear of raised voices, sarcasm, and profanities, which often alienate group members.

If some group members are reticent about particular topics, prompt them to respond. We sometimes have the tendency to assume silence equals agreement, but this is often not the case. Address the less-vocal members of your group for their reactions and opinions. Point out that the group would benefit from hearing from all group members. You may even elicit responses by stating, "Lee, we haven't heard from you yet. What are you thinking?" In situations where we might feel silenced, we would hope that our team members would ask for us to give our opinions or give us an opportunity to present our ideas. If you are hesitant to speak up during team meetings, challenge yourself to speak up. As Joanna Wolfe, the author of *Team Writing*, notes (Wolfe, 2010), if you are one of the first group members to speak, your team will start to see you as someone who has something to contribute.

If you have done your research, challenge yourself to share your ideas confidently and assertively.

5.2.5 Promote, but don't brag

On the opposite end of the spectrum from the timid group member is the braggart. Sometimes the bragging is subtle, but it is nevertheless irritating. In today's social-media driven world, narcissistic, self-promotional behaviors are rampant, where many use images of expensive cars, meals, and vacations to project a favorable image of themselves. However, psychology research (Marshall, Lefringhausen, & Ferenczi, 2015) suggests that those who often post to brag may actually be low in self-esteem. Other research (Scopelliti, Loewenstein, & Vosgerau, 2015) indicates that bragging behavior often elicits negative emotions from others.

We have seen bragging behavior negatively received both in the classroom and in the workplace. For example, we worked with a junior colleague who was enthusiastic and hard-working, but who used team meetings to brag about her professional accomplishments. This burgeoning "lone cowboy" talked about herself incessantly and "I" was her favorite word. On several occasions, she reminded us that she had been complimented for being a team player. The irony here was that this individual was quickly getting a reputation for being exactly the opposite of a team player. Eventually, we coached this member to use the pronoun "we" when talking about the work of the team. This simple fix created a less tense group environment. See Chapter 1 for more discussion of the importance of using the word "we" when discussing the work of the team.

What we suspect might have been at play for this colleague was her (mistaken) belief that bragging was necessary to build her credibility in the group. She might have confused bragging for self-promotion. Self-promotion, which can be important, is a more subtle, nuanced act. But even self-promotion can have adverse effects on the group. As Wolfe (2010) explains, "self-promotional talk often leads to hierarchical teams in which some work is perceived as more valuable … [and some group members] see themselves as immune to the criticisms and comments of the others" (p. 96). In our experience, self-promotion on teams should be used sparingly if at all.

In summary, saying that you worked on an award-winning research team might be appropriate to share with your team, or it might not. It would be appropriate (even helpful) to share this information if your intent is to share some best practices or lessons learned from the former team. It would be inappropriate if your intent is to illustrate how wonderful you are.

If you are put off by a group member's bragging, try to work past it by realizing that bragging is a sign of low self-confidence. If you are in the habit of extolling your own virtues, tone it down.

5.2.6 Capture diverse ideas

So often in groups, we see ideas being offered in rapid succession. This practice very often results in promising ideas being lost without any productive discussion of their merits or feasibility. Instead of immediately accepting (or more often) abandoning ideas presented by group members, try delving deeper into the ideas by asking questions to clarify the group members' ideas. The collective knowledge of a group is no help to the team unless it is shared and considered.

One tactic we teach groups to help them avoid losing ideas is to use the nominal group decision-making technique (Delbecq & VandeVen, 1971). The decision-making technique can be used to allow each group member's ideas to be succinctly presented and voted on and can work nicely when the group is at an impasse for how to move forward on a particular idea. There are several variations of the nominal group decision-making technique, but the version we practice involves group members privately writing down their individual ideas, then having one group member read them aloud. If questions arise, the person who contributed the idea is permitted to briefly (in one minute or less) explain it. After all ideas have been read (and explained, if necessary), we go around the table and have each group member state which solution they want to see implemented. The team then moves forward with the solution that received the most votes. We instruct the groups to retain all ideas for future reference.

Another tactic for capturing diverse ideas is to collect individual opinions at certain points during the process. Emmerling and Rooders (2020) recommend gathering individual opinions before people share their thoughts with the wider group. They suggest an iterative process in which team members first anonymously record their ideas in a shared document, then individually and anonymously assess the proposed ideas. These authors state that by following such a process, team members can counter biases and resist groupthink. This process, as they explain, ensures that "perceived seniority, alleged expertise, or hidden agendas don't play a role in what the group decides to do" (para. 7). We understand that this process is a bit time-consuming, and as such, your team might not be able to use it regularly. However, it can be quite helpful at critical or difficult points in your discussions.

Create a process for recording and capturing ideas. The loudest or most confident voice doesn't necessarily have the best idea.

5.2.7 Explore ideas

When a group sets out to solve a problem, it is not uncommon for them to assume there is only one right answer to that problem. However, if there really were only one correct answer, then a subject matter expert (instead of a group) would be the far better (and easier and faster) option than a group. There are often several viable methods to solving a problem. Once you have captured diverse ideas, it is time to further explore and test them.

One way to test (or challenge) the strength of an idea is to play devil's advocate. Playing **devil's advocate** means that you intentionally present a contentious opinion to provoke debate of the original idea. In fact, one study on the impact of using the devil's advocacy technique for team decision making (Waddell, Roberto, & Yoon, 2013) found that this technique helped groups achieve higher quality decisions than groups under free discussion. In another case study (Hartwig, 2010), the devil's advocacy technique was found to help group members develop a deeper understanding of an important problem.

At times, a group might appear committed to a particular course of action, but if you probe a bit deeper, you will discover that, in fact, the entire group is not on board. It is not uncommon for groups to mistake one or two vocal group members repeating the same ideas for group consensus. What this looks like is one or two group members dominating a conversation with their ideas, and other group members appearing to be in agreement. However, you should realize that the non-vocal group members may not actually agree with the proposed ideas; rather, they may be merely acquiescing or taking the path of least resistance in the group. These group members are just as likely to consider an alternative course of action. In situations like this, it is possible to bring other group members around to your ideas.

In our work with groups, we have seen "minority" opinions expressed and adopted in several teams. A tactic we have used in such situations is to concede that the original idea is "interesting" or "an option," but that you see an alternative option, and then present the alternative option. The key to persuading fellow group members is to present your alternative idea assertively and confidently.

Encourage your group members to discuss alternatives and be prepared to address questions they may have.

5.3 Remote and technological considerations

As we discussed in Chapter 3, online communication via channels such as Zoom and Microsoft Teams may present an extra layer of challenge in that it can be more difficult to read each other's nonverbal language. Although it may be distracting, we recommend that you keep your image on the screen so that you can monitor the non-verbal signals you are sharing. For instance, we have noticed that when we are in deep thought, we both take on expressions that others sometimes read as "distressed." Being able to see your own image allows you to correct any unintentional nonverbal signals.

During online meetings, some group members may choose to unmute themselves to speak while others may type their ideas and responses in the chat. For this reason, it is important to keep the chat open and have at least one group member monitor the chat during the meeting. We have participated in many online meetings where ideas that are posted in chat are missed or not addressed until much later. When this happens, it is sometimes difficult to recall what a particular chat comment is responding to. Therefore, if you are the facilitator make sure that you read the chat messages (that are intended for everyone) out loud to ensure that no comments go unnoticed.

We also found that often, team members benefit from knowing beforehand what you plan to share at the meeting. We have both walked into meetings and were presented with new ideas that we were expected to respond to right away. If your team members have not heard of your ideas yet, consider sending them a brief summary before the meeting to allow them to "process" your ideas.

5.4 Summary

This chapter explains the following key points about sharing ideas in group collaboration:

- When presenting your ideas (either in writing or in person), be as concise as possible.
- Instead of only offering new ideas, build on the ideas of others.
- Build your confidence by researching and gathering data to support your ideas.
- Recognize that bragging (by yourself or others) is often a sign of low self-confidence.
- Capture, discuss, and evaluate ideas from all team members.

5.5 Discussion questions

1. Do you have any experience developing or using an elevator speech? If so, when did you use it? If not, when might it be helpful to you?
2. How assertive are you in group meetings? Do you think you need to be more or less assertive? Why?
3. How might you be able to solicit feedback from group members who are typically quiet in meetings?
4. Do you have any experience linking your ideas to other ideas offered in a group? If so, how did the group members react to this?
5. How might you be able to ensure that your group captures and considers diverse ideas?

5.6 Activities

5.6.1 Building solution

This activity can be done either online or in-person. It asks students to respond to a problem and then to build a solution.

Object: The object of this activity is to respond to a problem and build on the ideas of others.

Setup: Every person should have a full sheet of paper and a writing instrument at the start of the activity.

Activity:

1. Each person should think about a problem that either they or someone they know has. They should pose that problem as a question on one side of the paper.

   Example: *How do I clean my clothes now that my washing machine is broken?*

2. Everyone should then pass their card to the right. The person who receives the problem should consider the problem and write a brief solution on the back of the page.

   Example: *Find the nearest laundromat.*

3. Everyone should again pass their card to the right. The person who receives the card should read the problem and the proposed solution, then **add to** the solution.

   Example: *Use the laundromat until you can afford a new washing machine.*

4. Once again, everyone should pass their card to the right. The person who receives the card should read the problem and the proposed solution, then **add to** the solution.

Example: *Save money for a new washing machine by making coffee at home instead of buying it every morning.*

5. Return the completed page to the person who posed the problem to review.

Post-activity discussion questions:

1. How easy or difficult was it to add to an existing solution? Would it have been easier to create something from scratch?
2. How could you use this activity during an actual group project?

Take-away: When you accept and build on the ideas of others, you can come up with some interesting and detailed solutions.

5.6.2 Tagline

This activity helps group members actively and visibly summarize their ideas to be more concise.

Object: The object of this in-person or online activity is to write a 30-second elevator speech and then to condense that speech into a five-word tagline.

Activity:

1. Every person should write a full paragraph self-introduction. Consider including anything professional, personal, or otherwise that you are comfortable sharing (7 minutes).

   Example: My name is Max, and I was newly hired on by the company to work in the distribution center. My work background includes grill and maintenance work in quick-service restaurants, and I am looking forward to a change of scenery! My favorite vacation spot is Vermont (on the New Hampshire side). In the spring and summer months, there are honeybees everywhere there.

2. Group members should be put in groups of three. Once grouped, the first group member should read their paragraph aloud. The group member who sits to the right of the person who read their paragraph is responsible for coming up with a 4–5 word tagline that best summarizes what that person said (3 minutes)

   Example: New hire likes bees.

3. The next group member should then share their full paragraph, and the person to their right is responsible for coming up with a 4–5 word tagline that best summarizes what that person said. And so forth (6 minutes).

Post-activity discussion questions:

1. What was easy, and what was difficult about summarizing someone else's paragraph?
2. How accurate was the tagline created for you? How was it different from what you might have created for yourself?

Take-away: Practicing summarizing your ideas will help you effectively share with others.

References

Biali Haas, S. (2019). Five essentials to help you speak with more confidence. *Psychology Today*, December 5. www.psychologytoday.com/us/blog/prescriptions-life/201912/five-essentials-help-you-speak-more-confidence.

Cahn, D. D., & Abigail, R. A. (2014). *Managing conflict through communication*. Pearson.

Costa, A. C., Fulmer, C. A., & Anderson, N. R. (2018). Trust in work teams: An integrative review, multilevel model, and future directions. *Journal of Organizational Behavior*, 39(2), 169–184. https://doi.org/10.1002/job.2213.

Covey, S. M. R., & Merrill, R. R. (2006). *The speed of trust: The one thing that changes everything*. Free Press.

Delbecq, A. L., & VandeVen, A. H (1971). A group process model for problem identification and program planning. *Journal of Applied Behavioral Science*. 7: 466–491. https://doi.org/10.1177/002188637100700404.

Devito, J. A. (2019). *The interpersonal communication book*. Pearson.

Emmerling, T., & Rooders, D. (2020). 7 strategies for better group decision-making. *Harvard Business Review*, September 22. https://hbr.org/2020/09/7-strategies-for-better-group-decision-making.

Erudera College News. (2021). Women outnumber men in US colleges—Nearly 60% of students in 2020/21 were women. *College News*, September 10. https://collegenews.org/women-outnumber-men-in-us-colleges-nearly-60-of-students-in-2020-21-were-women/.

Hartwig, R. T. (2010). Facilitating problem solving: A case study using the devil's advocacy technique. *Group Facilitation*, 10, 17–31.

Hellman, P. (2017). *You've got 8 seconds: Communication secrets for a distracted world*. American Management Association.

Levi, D. & Askay, D. A. (2021). *Group dynamics for teams*. Sage.

Marshall, T. C., Lefringhausen, K., & Ferenczi, N. (2015). The Big Five, self-esteem, and narcissism as predictors of the topics people write about in Facebook status updates. *Personality and Individual Differences*, 85, 35–40. https://doi.org/10.1016/j.paid.2015.04.039.

Roberts, D. (n.d.). The simple secret to establishing trust in your relationships at work and home. www.inc.com/debra-roberts/the-simple-secret-to-establishing-trust-in-your-relationships-at-work-home.html.

Scopelliti, I., Loewenstein, G., & Vosgerau, J. (2015). You call it "self-exuberance"; I call it "bragging": Miscalibrated predictions of emotional responses to self-promotion. *Psychological Science*, 26(6), 903–914. https://doi.org/10.1177/0956797615573516.

Turkle, S. (2016). *Reclaiming conversation: The power of talk in the digital age*. Penguin.

Waddell, B. D., Roberto, M. A., & Yoon, S. (2013). Uncovering hidden profiles: Advocacy in team decision making. *Management Decision*, 51(2), 321–340. https://doi.org/10.1108/00251741311301849.

Wolfe, J. (2010). *Team Writing: A Guide to Working in Groups*. Bedford St. Martin's.

6

EMPLOYING CREATIVITY

Questions to consider

- Are people more creative alone or in groups?
- What is the relationship between improvisation and creativity?
- What are some practices your group can use to build creativity?
- What benefits do constraints have on creativity?
- What is the relationship between context and group creativity?
- What impact does time have on group creativity?

6.1 Introduction to creativity

When people talk about creativity, they are sometimes referring to being skilled at various artistic forms such as music, painting, or writing. This is the reason we sometimes hear friends or colleagues lament that they don't have a creative bone in their body. But the root word of creativity is "create," which is to construct or build. Teams exist to construct or build products, processes, services, or solutions. In this sense, creativity is the work of teams. As such, creativity is highly valued in the workplace. A global CEO study conducted by IBM (2010) even found that creativity is the most crucial skill for future success. We certainly consider creativity to be extremely valuable in the teams we facilitate.

As collaboration researchers Beyerlein, Han, and Prasad (2018) aptly pointed out, "creativity does not occur in a vacuum. An enabling environment must exist" (p. 195). As we see it, the enabling environment starts with a team. To teach groups to be creative, we provide them with tools that enable them to "think outside the box" and encourage them to explore alternative methods of solving problems. Creativity will look different in every group, but it almost

DOI: 10.4324/9781003285571-7

always involves adopting a new perspective, finding a novel use for an existing item, or combining ideas or objects in new ways.

The benefits of employing creativity in groups is often the discovery of cost-effective or time-saving solutions to everyday challenges or unique responses to perplexing problems. These benefits will be evident in the solutions the group brings to the classroom and the workplace. In this chapter, we show you ways to become comfortable developing creative ideas. Before we do that, we'd like to address two points: the myth of the lone genius and the collaborative nature of creativity.

6.1.1 The myth of the lone genius

One of the biggest myths about creativity is the image of the lone genius. Think Albert Einstein or Steve Jobs. In reality, neither Einstein nor Jobs worked alone. Einstein collaborated with medical professionals like radiologist Gustav Bucky and medical doctor Hans Muhsam (Bucky & Einstein, 1935; Einstein & Muhsam, 1923). Steve Jobs's collaboration with Ed Catmull (computer scientist) and John Lasseter (animator and film director) resulted in Pixar evolving from a small film studio to a critically acclaimed cinematic computer animation studio (Catmull, 2008). In fact, it is difficult to think of an individual creative force who worked alone. Even great painters have their subjects.

Such partnerships illustrate that true creativity is typically the result of people with different backgrounds working together to create sometimes unbelievable results. These partnerships also show how the collaborative result is superior to the results that any of the individuals might have come up with independently. Research (e.g., Paulus & Nijstad, 2003; Sawyer, 2012) has long shown that when people are asked to devise creative solutions to real-world problems, teams outperform individuals.

6.1.2 The collaborative nature of creativity

Even if a project is seemingly simple or mundane, the creativity of the group can produce results that impact many. Take for instance, the hamburger wrapping patent. Patent WO2009126328A3 (Peyton et al., 2009) details a particular way of wrapping a special-order burger in paper and affixing a sticky "grill slip" (the piece of paper that indicates what the special order is) to the underside of the paper. The first part of the procedure was the initial brainchild of Arthur Peyton, who had years of experience working the grill and wrapping burgers via other methods. Arthur had the idea for a new wrapping procedure that was faster and more efficient, but he needed to be able to explain it to others. So, he sought the help of a technical writer to observe and break down what he was actually doing and write up a description of the process. During this process, which involved the technical writer asking detailed questions, Peyton fine-tuned his process. During this time, Peyton and the technical writer collaborated with two additional team members, both of whom had the restaurant technology and shift manager experience to help refine the initial process so that the wrapper could accommodate the sticky grill slip. This "simple" innovation changed the way thousands of restaurant workers across the US were taught to wrap their burgers. This example shows how even a seemingly "simple" idea (for wrapping a burger) can be enhanced through the creativity of a group.

Starting in the 1990s, a great deal of research was conducted on the collaborative nature of creativity. Several researchers have found that groups are fundamental to creativity. In other words, creativity is a social endeavor, requiring more than one individual. So, when it comes to matters of creativity, two heads are clearly better than one. As Sawyer and DeZutter (2009) explain, even studies of individual creators "have revealed a high level of collaboration behind their ideas" (p. 81). But, groups do more than expand the creativity past that of an individual. Groups are also responsible for the innovations that result from that creativity.

6.2 Practices for group creativity

Even if you might not consider yourself to be naturally creative, you can develop your creativity, particularly if you are in a group. In this chapter, we provide you with several practices to help your team use creativity.

6.2.1 Brainstorm

Brainstorming is the process of generating lots of ideas in a short amount of time. The idea is to simply amass ideas without prematurely judging them. Brainstorming is especially effective with groups, as our imaginations are often sparked by the ideas of others. Osborn's (1963) four tenets of making brainstorming effective are still useful today. These four principles are: deferring judgment, generating many ideas, encouraging unusual ideas, and combining ideas. We have noticed that these principles nicely align with the four principles of improv, which we describe in the introduction to this text.

When we facilitate brainstorming sessions in our classrooms and meetings, we start by giving prompts (often provocative in nature, as suggested by Seelig, 2012), such as stating, "It is the year 2052; this city is underwater" or "There are no laws in this country." These prompts encourage students to "think outside the box" or remove any artificial barriers they may be creating while they are germinating ideas. Just because an infrared robot waste collector can't fly behind your dog and pick up his droppings now, doesn't mean it won't ever happen. In fact, Bill Gates's 15 predictions in 1999, including smartphones and social media, have all been realized today (Weinberger, 2019).

Sometimes groups embark upon brainstorming sessions but do not take them far enough. In other words, they allow just a short amount of time to accumulate ideas but don't push past common or expected ideas. We generally limit brainstorming sessions to five minutes or fewer. If this seems like too little time for your particular problem, try breaking the problem down into smaller elements and brainstorming each element for five minutes or less. Alternatively, you could do two or more rounds of rapid brainstorming (three minutes or fewer per round). Engaging in rapid rounds of brainstorming is also referred to as brainstorming in waves (Seelig, 2012). The practice of brainstorming in waves forces team members to push past their initial ideas by implementing a second and a third wave of brainstorming sessions immediately following the first round. The reason for the multiple iterations is that more unusual or novel ideas often come later in brainstorming sessions, after all the usual ideas have been offered up.

Make brainstorming a regular part of your team process.

6.2.2 Accept ideas and build upon them

To ensure that all group members participate in brainstorming activities that we discuss above, group members should not criticize ideas during the brainstorming or other creative processes. Accepting ideas and building upon them is very similar to the improvisation practice of "just saying yes" that we cover in the introduction chapter. Our group brainstorming sessions start with rally cries such as, "Let's get as many ideas out as we can. Remember, every idea is a great idea!"

When you are working on a team, you may hear ideas that you immediately dismiss for some reason or another. Research shows that it is a human tendency to be skeptical and to reject or deny ideas that do not immediately align with our views or values. In fact, there is a very strong historical precedent for skepticism about new ideas. Prevailing wisdom in the Middle Ages was that the Earth was the center of the solar system. Copernicus presented an alternative idea: that the sun was at the center of the solar system. Hundreds of years later and based on newer technology, this idea was supported by Galileo. Galileo's championing of Copernicus's idea famously led to Galileo's trial for heresy—even though the idea turned out to be true.

If you have talked to skeptics before, you have probably already noticed that this is not a productive team practice. To optimize your group's creativity, instead of shooting novel ideas down or thinking of reasons they can't work, try to build on these ideas. Sometimes, we hastily rush to judgment on an idea we don't agree with or fully understand. Maintaining the "Yes, and …" mindset that characterizes improvisational games is critical to group creativity. Instead of telling your team member that her idea to institute a work from home option will never work, try to think of reasons that it might work. At the end of the day, the idea may not fly. But that's not the important point. To devise creative solutions, you often must suspend your initial judgment.

If three competing ideas are expressed equally as passionately, what is to keep the group from trying to adopt elements of each of the ideas? Nothing! If there is a way to harness this energy (or synergy), this might lead to the most creative or best of all possible outcomes.

Activity 6.6.1 provides an exercise that will allow you to practice building on the ideas of others.

Instead of rejecting an unfamiliar idea right away, try to accept the idea and build upon it.

6.2.3 Make observations

Observation (along with surveys and interviews) is a primary research method to gather data from participants in research studies. Observation is also key to many occupations and activities. Take the work of a user experience professional. This is a person who conducts usability tests and observes representative users' actions and reactions to a specific product so that the user experience professional can identify **pain points**, which are areas with which the user has particular difficulty. But observations are also important to creativity. Baas et al. (2014) conducted four psychology studies and confirmed that there is a positive link between observation and creativity, in that those who possess strong observation skills were associated with increased flexible thinking.

One reason that observations are important to creativity is that observations allow us to accurately assess the present situation. Until we understand the present state of affairs, we will not have enough data to determine what actually constitutes an improvement. For instance, if we do not understand the work process of a group of people, anything we develop to help them with their job may be redundant (or even counterproductive) if it doesn't fit within the process that they follow.

One example that we use in the classroom to highlight this point is Tammy's experience creating a user guide for a new order entry system. Several years ago, Tammy was hired to document a new order entry system for distribution center employees. She spent time with the software developers who designed this multi-screen system and gave her access to a test system, where she practiced creating and canceling various types of orders and documented her findings in a user guide. After several weeks, the new user guide was delivered to the distribution center employees. Although it contained correct information, the user guide was a failure. The problem was that the information was not organized in the same manner in which the distribution center employees fulfilled orders. When Tammy was asked to "fix" the guide, her first step was to visit the distribution floor (which she had not previously done) and talk with the workers. Next, she observed the flow of their work. After these observations, she discovered a much more helpful way to reorganize the user guide so that it more accurately reflected the workflow of the distribution center employees. Observation is what helped this solution work for this client.

Observation is a powerful method for assessing situations and seeing connections.

6.2.4 Connect random pieces

Even if there don't appear to be any obvious connections between the ideas of various group members, you could suggest combining a couple of random ideas. Being able to connect and combine non-obvious ideas and objects is an exercise in creativity and the hallmark of innovation. Connecting ideas that do not naturally go together is also a major component of academic, scientific and industry research.

Through observation (discussed earlier in this chapter) you will be able to identify ideas that could be connected. Be that group member who is on the lookout for connections between random pieces. When members jump from one to the next idea without connecting the dots, ask if the two ideas are mutually exclusive. State that you don't want to see any potentially promising ideas be lost. Point out connections between the ideas of various members. For example, as instructors, we often encourage students to connect their (sometimes seemingly random) comment to what was offered earlier in the group. Our request might sometimes force the student to be creative "on the spot." This ability, which can be developed through practice, is known as **cognitive flexibility** (Scott, 1962), which is defined as your brain's readiness to switch concepts when responding to a situation.

Even if you don't immediately see the connection between ideas, think about how you can connect them. Random pieces include any information shared with the group that do not appear to naturally go together, Random pieces also include information about the past, present, and future. As Vygotsky (2004) claims, creativity is about reworking and combining elements of past experience to generate the new. Activity 6.6.2 provides an exercise that will allow you to practice connecting random ideas to build a cohesive picture.

Don't be afraid of connecting random pieces to explore different possibilities.

6.2.5 Ask a different question

Playwright Eugene Ionesco wrote, "It is not the answer that enlightens, but the question" (as quoted by Wells, 1997, p. 15). What a profound way to say that questions hold the power. Especially when it comes to creativity, the questions that we ask define the scope of possible answers. The answers are beholden to (or dependent on) the questions. For example, asking your teammates how the group can meet the installation date is going to yield a much different set of answers than had you asked, "What could *you* do to help us meet the deadline?"

Asking a different question can also mean thinking more broadly about an issue. Consider the case of Amazon.com, which in the 1990s was only an online bookseller. Jeff Bezos, the founder and previous CEO, had the motto of "get big fast," (History, 2016), which prompted him and his team to ask a different question. The question Bezos and his team asked was, "What else can we sell to get big fast?" So, the company continued heavy expansion by moving from selling books to becoming one of the world's largest retailers.

Another question to ask is, "What or who else?" For instance, when we discuss **needs assessments** (the process of determining information about the needs of a particular population) with our student groups, we emphasize the importance of considering all potential **stakeholders** (people who will be impacted by the work we are doing).

In one activity, we ask our students to design a new city park, and we point out the daycare center next door to the proposed park. We don't specifically tell students that there is a retirement home on the other side of the park, but we do include information about the retirement home in some supplementary materials about the neighborhood. So, the students typically design their needs assessment considering only the children and their caregivers. By the next class meeting, we see if any of the groups have included anything in their needs assessment that considers the seniors' perspectives. Those groups (if any!) who considered the perspectives of the seniors will have necessarily asked different questions in their needs assessment. These questions (and their answers) will yield a very different type of the park than the one designed with only the daycare in mind.

Asking a different (not-so-obvious) question can help you approach your situation in a different way.

6.2.6 Ask a different type of expert

Just as asking a different question can lead to finding creative solutions, so too can asking a different expert. By different expert we mean someone whose field or occupation is different from your own. People in different fields often have different **paradigms**, or ways of making sense of the world. A person with a paradigm that drastically differs from you necessarily sees different systems, networks, and rules at play in their world. For instance, a pessimist could blame Murphy's Law (which is the observation that anything that can go wrong will go wrong) for her recent unseen car repair bill. A mechanic might see the same repair as evidence of poor car maintenance. Always remember that people with different backgrounds than ours can help us find different answers.

To whom would you go to determine if the painting you scored at the thrift store is an original or a fake? Perhaps you would go to an art dealer or an art historian. But you might be better off going to a physicist. It turns out that a physicist can tell from the isotopes in the paint just how old a piece of artwork is. Isotopes are atoms that have similar chemical properties but different mass or physical properties. It turns out that the presence of two specific isotopes—cesium 137 and strontium 90—indicate that a painting may be a forgery. The thing is, these particular isotopes didn't exist prior to the first nuclear tests and were absorbed by the plants used to produce paints after 1945. According to the scientists who came up with this idea, if artwork purporting to have been painted prior to 1945 is found via testing to use paints which contain caesium-137 and strontium-90, there's a high probability that it's a forgery.

We decide what our problem is by choosing the type of "expert" on whom we call. In this sense, the answer to your problem depends on whom you ask. For instance, let's say you have a backache. If you ask a chiropractor, the answer is a spinal adjustment. If you ask a massage therapist, the answer is a massage. If you ask your doctor, the answer may be a pill. Is the problem with your dog medical, behavioral, or emotional? The answer will depend on whether you visit a veterinarian, a trainer, or a psychic.

One way that you can ask a different type of expert is by expanding your network. Your professional network could include your professors and classmates, your colleagues at work, or alumni from your high school or college. We have found that serving on cross-functional teams or joining student clubs can help introduce you to people outside of your immediate professional and social circles. By interacting with others who have different knowledge and skills, you will likely get a different perspective than your own.

Think about whom you can talk with to get a different viewpoint.

6.2.7 Impose constraints

Although constraints are sometimes perceived to be negative (e.g., budget or time constraints), we have found that constraints, both in the workplace and in the classroom, can actually encourage teams to be creative, as they force your brain to reorganize information and select only details that are important.

For example, our students often present their projects using the PechaKucha (Japanese word for "chit-chat") method. This method was created in 2003 by two architects, Astrid Klein and Mark Dytham, who wanted their colleagues to be efficient and effective with their presentations, so they limited the number of slides to 20, and each slide advances automatically after 20 seconds. This method is also known as 20 × 20, and the entire presentation can last for only six minutes and 40 seconds (PechaKucha, n.d.). Initially, some students struggle with the idea of "fitting" 20 seconds worth of speech into each slide, but they eventually learn that this method forces them to be more creative and concise with their words. For example, instead of reading verbatim from their report, which they tend to do when reporting on their project results, students learn to paraphrase and summarize their results using easy-to-understand and colloquial terms.

Constraints are often what prompt your team to make forward progress and avoid "analysis paralysis," which can happen when you are given a large nebulous task and there are limitless directions you can go. Think about common constraints used on popular social media platforms. For example, Twitter limits the number of characters for each tweet to 280, while TikTok videos are limited to three minutes. Users are forced to be creative about the words or the length of words that they put on their tweet, or they have to edit their TikTok video content more creatively or carefully.

In terms of the impact of constraints on workplace creativity, Rosso (2014) studied research and development teams in multinational corporations and confirmed that "teams experiencing the right kinds of constraints in the right environments, and which saw opportunity in constraints, benefitted creatively from them" (p. 551). More specifically, the perception of constraints plays an important role for the team. If the team interprets the constraints they face as being able to enhance team creativity, then they are more likely to benefit from the constraints.

An example of a constraint you could introduce to your team is to ask, "Could we all agree that since we have three ideas to review in one hour, that we spend 20 minutes focusing on each?" Even if it's only at a subconscious level, some team members will work a bit more rapidly given the time constraint.

If your team is not given any constraints, try to immediately establish some.

6.2.8 Select a space that works

Creativity is more than a group following processes and observing constraints. Creativity can also be enhanced through the context or setting of a group. **Contexts** involve the physical space the group members are inhabiting (a classroom, a board room, a park); any media through which the group communicates; and any personal or social issues that may be occurring simultaneously around the group.

Let's first examine the physical space of the group. Many workplace elements, including furnishings, lighting, sounds, smells, and colors can foster creativity. This is the reason some organizations have dedicated creative spaces. These spaces often include resources such as whiteboards, colored markers, and sticky notes to support a team's creative processes. Research (Christensen, Halskov, & Klokmose, 2020; Inouye, Bae, & Hayes, 2017) shows that using such resources can enhance creative thinking. Because some physical spaces (such as classrooms) can be cramped, overly-lit, and not conducive to collaboration, we sometimes suggest that groups choose an alternative location to work together. Sometimes, groups choose to go into empty lab rooms, common areas, or even outdoors.

Although organizational creativity can flourish in all types of spaces, spatial designs in the workplace need to "give space for spontaneous creativity to emerge" (De Paoli & Ropo, 2017, p. 162). Similarly, Sicotte et al. (2019) found that the arrangement of space in the workplace affects employee's sense of belonging, which in turn can influence both team effectiveness and creativity. This is evident in successful companies like Google, Apple, and Facebook. For example, Google's Broadway-themed conference rooms and workstations that look like giant Tinker Toys show that they recognize the importance of creating a corporate environment that is conducive to creativity (Stewart, 2013).

In addition to the physical space, context also refers to any media through which the group communicates and collaborates. As more teams are meeting online via Zoom, Google Meet, or Microsoft Teams, there are online tools that can be used to brainstorm their ideas on the same page. Refer to section 6.3 below for remote and technological considerations related to employing group creativity.

Finally, context refers to any personal or social issues that may be occurring simultaneously around the group. For instance, context would include the facts that the globe is in the midst of a pandemic, and you are not as engaging with the group (because you are distracted by worries related to visiting your elderly, unvaccinated grandmother).

Keep in mind the various ways that context impacts the thinking and work of the team.

6.2.9 Dedicate an appropriate amount of time

While some people are comfortable verbally contributing dozens of unique responses in a few minutes (recall the brainstorming practice described earlier), others prefer to let their ideas germinate and are more comfortable articulating these ideas when they are more fully formed.

For this reason, it is an effective practice to introduce an idea in a meeting, but to ask for responses the next day or during the next meeting. In fact, research (Wagner et al., 2004) shows that "sleeping on an idea" is beneficial, where sleep can improve our cognitive ability. In fact, there is substantial empirical support suggesting that sleep facilitates memory retention (Beijamini et al, 2014; Chambers, 2017) and creative problem-solving skills (e.g., Drago et al., 2011; Ritter et al., 2012; Yordanova et al., 2010). These findings suggest that we can potentially activate creativity-related processes during sleep and thereby boost the beneficial effect of sleep on creativity.

However, there is a limit to the time that we dedicate to a problem. As you might imagine, at some point, more time does not equate to more, better ideas. In fact, Baer and Oldham's (2006) study shows an inverted U-shaped relation between experienced creative time pressure and creativity, where employees showed more creativity when they "experienced intermediate creative time pressure and received considerable support for creativity from supervisors and coworkers" (p. 968). We have similarly found that applying time constraints motivates team members to push through their natural, but obstructive self-monitoring.

We start most of our brainstorming sessions and other group meetings with a statement reminding everyone of the goals for the meeting and the amount of time we have available. Refer to Chapter 9 for additional guidance for group meetings.

Dedicating an appropriate amount of time to developing ideas and completing tasks can improve creativity.

6.3 Remote and technological considerations

As mentioned earlier, physical sticky notes (along with markers and flipcharts) are found to be useful in generating creative ideas. Similarly, digital tools that can be used online, such as Mural, can assist teams in capturing their ideas. Mural is a digital white board tool that allows team members to capture ideas on digital "sticky notes," group them, and reorganize them. Jensen et al. (2018) found that both physical and digital methods help with the collaborative ideation process, but the digital version invites more interaction. This may be because some group members who are hesitant to contribute verbally may have an easier time doing so electronically.

If your group meetings will be held online or virtually, there are several additional websites or tools that your team could use to make the meeting more effective for exploring creative ideas or projects. For instance, Figma is a widely used collaborative design tool that companies use to manage or streamline their design process or workflow. Figma's clients include Airbnb, Netflix, and Zoom (Konrad, 2021). This tool allows you and your team members to brainstorm ideas and design visuals such as maps and diagrams synchronously or in real time. It now has a built-in application that allows team members to meet online while they work on the same design project.

Another online tool that can help you share ideas and images with your team members is the electronics moodboard creator application, GoMoodBoard.com. This tool allows you to build electronic collages of digital images and words to share with your team members. Google's Jamboard is another tool for brainstorming ideas synchronously with your team members.

6.4 Summary

This chapter explains the following key points about employing creativity in group collaboration:

- Begin brainstorming sessions with provocative prompts.
- Make observations or pay closer attention to details.
- Accept ideas (even if they may sound unreasonable at first) and build upon them.
- Connect random pieces or dots to develop your cognitive flexibility.
- Ask a different question or a different expert and try to expand your network.
- Impose constraints on brainstorming sessions such as time and context.

6.5 Discussion questions

1. Besides what is mentioned in this chapter, what additional creativity tools have you found to be effective in team meetings?
2. Where or when do you find yourself having the most "aha!" moments?
3. What is your biggest hurdle when it comes to being creative?

4. Do you have any experience connecting random ideas? In what situations has (or could) this technique be useful?
5. What are your favorite places to work as a team? Besides your usual meeting place, where else might your team be able to meet to best collaborate?

6.6 Activities

6.6.1 Solving an intergalactic problem

This in-person activity asks students to respond to fictional problems that are not bound by laws of space or time. In the activity, students will gain experience building on the ideas of others while adhering to specific constraints.

Object: The object of this game is to work independently, but collaboratively, to solve random problems that might occur in worlds other than our own.

Setup: Group members should assemble in groups of four. Each group member should have a piece of paper and a pencil. Ask students to independently come up with a problem that is faced by the inhabitants of a newly discovered planet in a newly discovered galaxy.

Activity: This activity consists of four parts and a debrief:

Part I Each person should come up with a specific problem that is faced by the inhabitants of a newly discovered planet in a newly discovered galaxy. Individuals should note this problem on the top of a piece of paper. The problem should be as specific as possible. For instance, the problem could be that inhabitants are running low on the natural resource that is used to heat their homes. After the problem is articulated, each person should pass their question to the person on their right.

Part II Each person should take a few minutes to review the problem with which they are presented. They should then write a couple of lines suggesting how to solve that problem. After four minutes are up, have each student pass their papers to the person on their right.

Part III Each person should take a few minutes to review the new problem with which they are presented and to read the initial idea about how to solve that problem. They should then build upon that idea by writing 3–4 additional lines of explanation for solving the problem. After four minutes are up, have each student pass their question to the person on their right. Repeat this step until the piece of paper is back at the originator of the question.

Part IV The person who posed the question should read through the entire proposed solution aloud, and the group should evaluate its strengths.

Take-away: Having constraints can help you find more creative solutions.

6.6.2 I am a tree

This in-person activity asks group members to visualize a scene and to let that scene evolve as other group members build it real-time. In the activity, people will gain experience adjusting to an evolving group vision and building on the ideas of others.

Object: The object of this game is to create a static scene or picture with the entire group.

Setup: Five-six "players" stand at either side of the room, just off the "stage" area. The other group members should sit as audience members, facing the players.

Activity: The first player comes "center stage" and indicates what he or she is. For instance, the player may lift her arms out to his sides and state, "I am a tree." The next player adds to this scene by joining the first player on stage and stating what he is. For instance, he might sit under the "tree" and say, "I am the apple that has fallen from the tree." The third player joins in by stating what she is. "I am a picnic basket left near the apple," and so on. Once the fifth player has explained what he is, the sixth player starts a new scene by tapping out one player, assuming that position (for instance, he may tap out the apple), and say, "I am an apple." All other players leave the stage, and begin to build a new scene around this item.

Take-away: This game forces group members to listen, to make connections between ideas, and to visualize a static story.

References

History. (2021). Amazon opens for business. July 14. www.history.com/this-day-in-history/amazon-opens-for-business.

Baas, M., Nevicka, B., & ten Velden, F. (2014). Specific mindfulness skills differentially predict creative performance. *Personality & Social Psychology Bulletin*, 40(9), 1092–1106. https://doi.org/10.1177/0146167214535813.

Baer, M., & Oldham, G. R. (2006). The curvilinear relation between experienced creative time pressure and creativity: Moderating effects of openness to experience and support for creativity. *Journal of Applied Psychology*, 91(4), 963–970. https://doi.org/10.1037/0021-9010.91.4.963.

Beijamini, F., Pereira, S. I. R., Cini, F. A., & Louzada, F. M. (2014). After being challenged by a video game problem, sleep increases the chance to solve it. *PloS One*, 9(1), e84342–e84342. https://doi.org/10.1371/journal.pone.0084342.

Beyerlein, M., Han, S. J., & Prasad, A. (2018). A multilevel model of collaboration and creativity. In R. Reiter-Palmon (Ed.), *Team creativity and innovation* (pp. 195–224). Oxford University Press.

Bucky, G., & Einstein, A. (1935). Light intensity self-adjusting camera. US Patent No. 2058562A, US Patent and Trademark Office. https://patents.google.com/patent/US2058562A/en.

Catmull, E. (2008). How Pixar fosters collective creativity. *Harvard Business Review*, September. https://hbr.org/2008/09/how-pixar-fosters-collective-creativity.

Chambers, A. M. (2017). The role of sleep in cognitive processing: focusing on memory consolidation. *Cognitive Science*, 8(3). https://doi.org/10.1002/wcs.1433.

Christensen, B. T., Halskov, K., & Klokmose, C. N. (2020). *Sticky creativity: Post-it note cognition, computers, and design*. Elsevier.

Coleman, A. (2016). Is Google's model of the creative workplace the future of the office? *The Guardian*, February 11. www.theguardian.com/careers/2016/feb/11/is-googles-model-of-thecreative-workplace-the-future-of-the-office.

De Paoli, D. & Ropo, A. (2017). Creative workspaces—a fad or making real impact? *Journal of Corporate Real Estate*, 19(3), 157–166.

Drago, V., Foster, P. S., Heilman, K. M., Aricò, D., Williamson, J., Montagna, P., & Ferri, R. (2011). Cyclic alternating pattern in sleep and its relationship to creativity. *Sleep Medicine*, 12(4), 361–366. https://doi.org/10.1016/j.sleep.2010.11.009.

Dul, J., & Ceylan, C. (2011). Work environments for employee creativity. *Ergonomics*, 54(1), 12–20. https://doi.org/10.1080/00140139.2010.542833.

Einstein, A., & Muhsam, H. (1923). Experimentelle Bestimmung der Kanalweite von Filtern. *Deutsch Medizin Wochensch*, 49, 1012–1013.

IBM. (2010). 2010 global CEO study: Creativity selected as most crucial factor for future success. www.ibm.com/news/ca/en/2010/05/20/v384864m81427w34.html.

Inouye, C., Bae, C. L., & Hayes, K. N. (2017). Using whiteboards to support college students' learning of complex physiological concepts. *Advances in Physiology Education*, 41(3), 478–484. https://doi.org/10.1152/advan.00202.2016.

Jensen, M. M., Thiel, S. K., Hoggan, E., & Bødker, S. (2018). Physical versus digital sticky notes in collaborative ideation. *Computer Supported Cooperative Work: CSCW: An International Journal*, 27(3–6),609–645. https://doi.org/10.1007/s10606-018-9325-1, https://doi.org/10.1007/s10606-018-9325-1.

Konrad, A. (2021). How Figma became design's hottest startup, valued at $10 billion. Forbes, August 10. www.forbes.com/sites/alexkonrad/2021/08/10/how-figma-became-designs-hottest-startup-valued-at-10billion/?sh=69365994726e.

Osborn, A. F. (1963). *Applied imagination: Principles and procedures of creative problem-solving*. New York: Scribner.

Paulus, P. B. & Nijstad, B. A. (Eds.). (2003). *Group creativity: Innovation through collaboration*. New York: Oxford University Press.

Pechakucha. (n.d.). About us. Retrieved on January 4, 2022. www.pechakucha.com/about.

Peyton, A., Rice-Bailey, T., Blanchard, S., & Nascimento, A. (2009). Packaged food product and method of packaging and identifying packaged products. US Patent No. WO2009126328A3, US Patent and Trademark Office. https://patents.google.com/patent/WO2009126328A3.

Ritter, S. M., Strick, M., Bos, M. W., Van Baaren, R. B., & Dijksterhuis, A. P. (2012). Good morning creativity: Task reactivation during sleep enhances beneficial effect of sleep on creative performance. *Journal of Sleep Research*, 21(6), 643–646. https://doi.org/10.1111/j.1365-2869.2012.01006.x.

Rosso, B. D. (2014). Creativity and constraints: Exploring the role of constraints in the creative processes of research and development teams. *Organization Studies*, 35(4). https://doi.org/10.1177%2F0170840613517600.

Sawyer, R. K. (2012). *Explaining creativity: The science of human innovations*. Oxford University Press.

Sawyer, R. K., & DeZutter, S. (2009). Distributed creativity: How collective creations emerge from collaboration. *Psychology of Aesthetics, Creativity, and the Arts*, 3(2), 81–92. https://doi.org/10.1037/a0013282.

Scott, W. A. (1962). Cognitive complexity and cognitive flexibility. *Sociometry*, 25(4), 405–414. https://doi.org/10.2307/2785779.

Seelig, T. (2012). *inGenius: A crash course on creativity*. HarperCollins.

Sicotte, H., De Serres, A., Delerue, H., & Ménard, V. (2019). Open creative workspaces impacts for new product development team creativity and effectiveness. *Journal of Corporate Real Estate*, 21(4), 290–306. https://doi.org/10.1108/JCRE-10-2017-0039.

Stewart, J. B. (2013). Looking for a lesson in Google's perks. *The New York Times*, March 15. www.nytimes.com/2013/03/16/business/at-google-aplace-to-work-and-play.html.

Vygotsky, L. S. (2004). Imagination and creativity in childhood. *Journal of Russian and East European Psychology*, 42(1): 7–96.

Wagner, U., Gais, S., Haider, H., Verleger, R. & Born, J. (2004). Sleep inspires insight. *Nature*, 427, 352–355.

Weinberger, M. (2019). Bill Gates made these 15 predictions back in 1999—and it's fascinating how accurate he was. *Business Insider*, January 30. www.businessinsider.com/bill-gates-15-predictions-in-1999-come-true-2017-6#no-15-business-community-software-15.

Wells, S. (1997). *Choosing the future: The power of strategic thinking*. Routledge.

Yordanova, J., Kolev, V., Wagner, U., & Verleger, R. (2010). Differential associations of early- and late-night sleep with functional brain states promoting insight to abstract task regularity. *PloS One*, 5(2), e9442–e9442. https://doi.org/10.1371/journal.pone.0009442.

7

MANAGING CONFLICT

Questions to consider

- How can you provide and respond to constructive feedback?
- What is the difference between positions and interests, and why is this difference important?
- How might you address unproductive conflict?
- What can you say to a teammate who responds emotionally?
- How can you refocus and re-energize your team?

7.1 Introduction

When you are working on a team, the question is not whether you will encounter conflict, it is how you are going to handle the inevitable conflict that arises. Some conflict is relatively straightforward and commonplace. For instance, when you provide constructive feedback, you are effectively stating that you have a difference of opinion with a teammate. Other conflict is more complicated. This chapter examines various types of conflict that you might experience in your groups.

But first, a bit of background on the relationship between conflict and groups. Several decades ago, a group dynamics researcher, Bruce Tuckman (1965) found that conflict is a natural part of any group. Tuckman explained that groups develop in stages. Even today, group leaders rely on these four stages to talk about how groups develop. In the first stage (*forming*), group members test the boundaries of both interpersonal and task behaviors. Next, groups enter the *storming* stage, which is characterized by conflict, resistance, and polarization around interpersonal issues. In this stage, as the name suggests, conflict is most

DOI: 10.4324/9781003285571-8

evident. But the storming stage is also necessary for the final two stages, which are *norming* (cohesiveness starts developing) and finally *performing* (the group's energy is channeled into the work of the group). Tuckman found that not only was storming a normal part of the team building process, but also that the teams that avoided storming were much less successful than teams that used it as an opportunity to create supportive norms and expectations for members.

Group conflict is not inherently negative; it simply indicates that there are different people on the team, with different experiences and ideas. Working through the conflict and trying to reconcile it can often result in creative solutions. For instance, if you believe that Twitter is the best platform on which to promote your team's product, but other group members think that Tik Tok is better, you have a potential conflict. If, however, the team discusses the merits of both social media platforms and decides to put effort into both, this could be the beginning of a creative solution.

7.2 Practices for managing conflict

In our academic and workplace experience, we have identified productive ways to resolve various types of conflict.

7.2.1 Provide and accept constructive feedback

Let's face it: You will not think all ideas presented by your group members are great. For this reason, it is important to be able to provide constructive feedback.

To provide constructive feedback, start by explaining what works well or what you like about the idea you heard. Then, state what is problematic (if anything) about the idea. Next, indicate what questions remain for you about the idea. Be specific. A common mistake is to assume your group members know exactly what you are talking about. When you explain what information is missing or confusing, you allow the group member to fill in the blanks. Figure 7.1 shows group members reviewing and critiquing ideas the team has offered.

For instance, if a group member suggests that the group undertake a **SWOT Analysis** (which identifies the strengths, weaknesses, opportunities, and threats of a project), you might start by saying, "That's an interesting idea." But your feedback should not end there. You could follow up by stating that this type of analysis has potential for providing the team with insights, but that a SWOT analysis is typically better suited for companies considering their place in a competitive marketplace and not for limited scope projects. You might further note that a discussion about opportunities and threats could be interesting, but a conversation about strengths and weaknesses wouldn't be as productive with a limited scope project.

FIGURE 7.1 Reviewing and critiquing ideas

Epstein (2018) suggests additional tips for giving and receiving candid feedback. Among these are:

1. Give your teammates the benefit of the doubt. If they provide you with feedback, assume that they have your best interest in mind.
2. Don't talk about your teammates; talk directly with your teammates. Gossip usually doesn't improve a person's behavior. It is more effective to talk directly with the person whose behavior concerns you. This can resolve misunderstandings without creating drama or involving others.

You should also be gracious when a teammate gives you constructive feedback. If a team member challenges your idea, don't feel obligated to immediately defend it. It can be difficult to "think on your feet," and it's acceptable to tell your team members that you need time to think about their ideas. If your ideas or opinions are challenged, you can try saying:

- "That's an interesting perspective. Let me give it some consideration."
- "I feel like we're saying the same thing. Can you articulate how your idea differs from mine?"
- "I wonder if there are places where our ideas overlap."

When providing constructive feedback, start by letting your group member know what *does* work about their idea. When receiving constructive feedback, allow yourself time to respond.

7.2.2 Negotiate differences

Making decisions in a group is often a complicated endeavor. At times, your team will need to negotiate differences among team members. Let's say your group typically meets every Tuesday and Thursday afternoon, but you want to take a break from the project meetings during a holiday week. However, some other group members want to "power through" and meet during this notoriously quiet time. You might decide to "split the difference" and meet one time during the week. Is this compromise the optimal decision for anyone? Probably not. You might have planned a vacation over the break, and other group members might have family coming in from out of town. If you opt for the compromise, and meet just one of the days, none of you will get what you want.

So, what do you do? First, stop arguing for your position and second, start exploring your interests. Your **position** is akin to a demand. In our example, your position is, "I'm not meeting over the break." But, since this position is in conflict with the position of several other group members, you (and your group members) will have to dig a little deeper and look at the specific **interests** underlying your respective positions. Perhaps some of these group members who want to meet over the break are concerned that there will not be enough time to get the work done unless the team meets over the break. This concern constitutes their interest (which by-the-way, is not in conflict with your interest).

One of your primary interests is being able to take your vacation, but another of your interests is getting the work done. Instead of drawing a line in the sand, which is what asserting a position does, you could share your interests with your team members and ask them to share theirs. By sharing your interests (rather than demanding your positions), the group could come to a creative solution, such as meeting for an extra hour or two the week before the break.

For many group decisions, consensus is the optimal approach. However, consensus may not always be possible. Sometimes, team members have incompatible goals. For instance, if a team member believed that their department or livelihood could be jeopardized by the work of the team, they may have an incentive to stall or even scuttle the work of the group. Other times, team members might be incentivized to support an option other than the one that is garnering the most support.

When consensus is not achievable, the group will have to find ways to negotiate their differences. This will be much easier if the group already has a contract that states how it will make decisions. See Chapter 9 for more information on team contracts and making decisions as a group.

Learn to negotiate differences by exploring the interests that lie behind your positions.

7.2.3 Address unproductive conflict

Some conflict is unproductive. Let's say that two group members are arguing over a minor point. Whether it is a point of pride, a personality conflict, or something else, this conflict is not likely to end in a creative solution. If you observe or are a party to unproductive conflict in your team, we recommend that you address the conflict. Of course, how you address this conflict will depend on the situation and the issue. Unless you are experienced in handling conflict, or a group member's bad behavior is recurring, we suggest taking these conversations "offline"—meaning that you approach the group member (generally after the meeting) and tell them that you want to talk to them privately. You could say something like, "We need to talk about what happened in the meeting today." Then arrange a convenient time and place to talk. Cahn and Abigail, the authors of *Managing Conflict through Communication*, suggest that this conversation take place within 24 hours from when you spoke and that you select a place that is relatively private and free of distractions (Cahn & Abigail, 2014).

When you meet to discuss the conflict, try not to assess the motives or reasoning behind what another person has said. Remember, give them the benefit of the doubt. Instead of making assumptions, ask questions. It is also helpful to use I-statements. I-statements allow you to discuss issues without sounding like you are accusing or blaming the other person. I-statements force you to take ownership for your own perceptions and actions. Saying to a group member, "I am frustrated by your actions" shifts the emphasis to yourself. This type of I-statement also sounds less like criticism and minimizes the likelihood that the other person will respond defensively.

We also advise that when you are trying to resolve unproductive conflict, avoid telling the other person what to do. Telling someone what they "should" do can be perceived as condescending or bossy. It also negatively impacts that person's sense of autonomy. A better option is to share ideas for what they *might* do or *could* do. Instead of saying, "You should text or email if you are going to miss a meeting," try saying, "If you're going to miss a meeting, you could text or email the team."

If a team member persists with the bad behavior (perhaps condescending to you or interrupting you), you might choose to address this behavior immediately. Simply say something like, "Excuse me, Olivia, but you just cut me off. I would like to finish what I was saying…" A word of caution about calling out bad behavior in front of other team members: It might cause the team member to become defensive, and the conversation could devolve into counter-accusations or even insults. One of us has had the unfortunate experience of needing to intervene in a group where two members began to verbally assault each other. These situations are disruptive and uncomfortable for all group members.

When addressing unproductive conflict, focus on asking questions to get clarity, avoid telling the person what to do or how to feel, and act immediately if you notice a persistent pattern.

7.2.4 Address emotional reactions

What happens if a team member becomes emotional during a heated discussion? In these situations, we find it helpful for everyone to take a breath and then for someone (perhaps you!) to ask a few direct questions. We have used the following questions to try to work through emotional or inarticulate responses:

- "What is your biggest concern with this [course of action] or [solution]?"
- "Can you provide us with some texture around your [idea] or [concern]?"
- "What are we missing?"
- "What part of this isn't working for you?"

Once you have listened to their response, paraphrase the response to be sure you understand it and then ask additional clarifying questions as needed. Davey (2019) explains that once you think you have gotten to the root of the emotion, you can pivot your questions toward action. For instance, you could ask your team member, "What would a good path forward look like for you?" or "What would need to be included in our plan to address that concern?" Once the conversation shifts toward a plan, Davey explains, you will see the emotion dissipate.

Or, consider a situation where you were the emotional one in a meeting. If, after that meeting, you believe that you acted in a way that was not helpful, own up to it. Make an effort to repair any possible interpersonal damage that may have resulted from disagreements with your teammates, particularly if during those disagreements you behaved in a less-than-professional manner. Even in the workplace, there are CEOs who recognize the importance of handling disagreements openly and directly by instructing their employees to do it *in person* (Turkle, 2016).

Nawaz (2019) suggests that once you realize a discussion didn't go well, you should meet with your team member(s) and take accountability for what you did wrong. Ask them if they would be willing to discuss the incident and talk about how to avoid this type of incident in the future. Once you've apologized, Nawaz advises you "thank your colleague for their good intentions or any positive actions they took during the conversation, such as being a good listener while you ranted." This will show your team members that you recognize your weaknesses and want to improve on them. This will also clear the path for you to reemphasize the overall goals of the group and let your team members know you are committed to working collaboratively to these goals.

When you are involved in an emotional conflict with another team member, attempt to repair the relationship by asking questions to gain clarity and owning up to your behaviors.

7.2.5 Refocus

Teams have energy levels. Conflict, inability to give constructive feedback, emotional reactions, and lack of progress suck energy out of the team. Whenever you sense that there is a lack of energy on the team or the team feels stuck, it is time to refocus. One way to refocus is to try to gain some perspective about the current difficulties or lack of progress. Don't assume your fellow team members recognize the same dynamics that you see at play. Articulating your observation about the shifting team dynamics can be very useful, even if you think that your observations are obvious.

For instance, say that the team has been struggling over a major point and cannot come to an agreement about how to move forward. You observe that the same two group members make the same arguments at each meeting. It would be beneficial to the team if you pointed this out, and either (1) put the burden on those two team members to resolve the conflict outside of the team's time and ask them to present their solution for group approval at the next meeting, or (2) use the decision-making method you agreed to as a team (described in Chapter 9) to move beyond the disagreement.

A second way to refocus the team is to remind them of past successes at overcoming conflict or inertia. If your team has been struggling to complete a particular task and the group's morale is low, you might remind the team of a similar struggle it tackled and the positive results that were accomplished.

A third way to refocus the team is to remind team members of their common, shared goals and potential future successes. Lorelie Parolin, US learning lead and dean of Hamburger University for McDonald's Corporation describes a visioning activity (detailed in Activity 7.6.2) that she facilitates to reinvigorate her teams. In this activity, Parolin instructs each team member to imagine what success would look like in terms of a newspaper headline or an award title. She then asks them, "What would the headline read or what would the award say?" As Parolin explains, "This activity gets people excited; it realigns and reinvigorates the team."

If your team is struggling, try to remind them of their common purpose and end goals.

7.3 Remote and technological considerations

As we discussed in Chapter 3, online communication via channels such as Zoom and Microsoft Teams may present an extra layer of challenge in that it can be more difficult to read each other's nonverbal language. Although it may be distracting, we recommend that you keep your image on the screen so that you can monitor the non-verbal signals you are sharing. For instance, we have noticed that when we are in deep thought, we both take on expressions that others sometimes read as "distressed." Being able to see your own image allows you to correct any unintentional nonverbal signals.

During online meetings, some group members may choose to unmute themselves to speak while others may type their ideas and responses in the chat. Group members whose comments go unnoticed or unaddressed may become upset. For this reason, it is important to keep the chat open and have at least one group member monitor the chat during the meeting. We have participated in many online meetings where ideas that are posted in chat are missed or not addressed until much later. When this happens, it is sometimes difficult to recall what a particular chat comment is responding to. Therefore, if you are the facilitator make sure that you read the chat messages (that are intended for everyone) out loud to ensure that no comments go unnoticed.

We also found that often, team members benefit from knowing beforehand what you plan to share at the meeting. We have both walked into meetings and were presented with new ideas that we were expected to respond to right away. Sometimes unexpected topics can cause confusion or anxiety in your team members. If your team members have not heard of your ideas yet, consider sending them a brief summary before the meeting to allow them to "process" the ideas.

7.4 Summary

This chapter explains the following key points about creating a supportive environment:

- Let your group members know what works about their ideas before suggesting how they could change them.
- When receiving constructive feedback, allow yourself time to respond.
- Stop arguing for your position and start exploring your interests.
- When addressing unproductive conflict, focus on asking questions to gain clarity, but avoid telling your teammate what to do.
- Attempt to repair relationships by asking questions to gain clarity and owning up to your own behaviors.
- It is important for team members to remind each other of their common purpose and end goals.

7.5 Discussion questions

1. Think about the last time you provided constructive feedback to someone. How was it received by the other person? What was the end result?
2. Can you recall a time where had you argued for your interest (rather than a position) you would have been more successful?
3. Can you think of a situation where using I-statements could be helpful?
4. When was the last time you were in a difficult conversation? How did you handle it?
5. Think about a time when you observed conflict being handled poorly in a group. What did the group members do that seemed ineffective?
6. What are some ways you can focus on the positives of your group?

7.6 Activities

7.6.1 Positions and interests

This activity can be done either online or in-person. It asks students to explore the interests that lie behind their own position and the position of their partner and to attempt to come to a negotiated agreement.

Object: The object of this activity is to attempt to come to a negotiated agreement for a specific problem.

Setup: Team members are put into pairs, and each person should have paper and a writing utensil.

Activity:

1. Consider this scenario: You and your partner share a car. Your position is that you want to use the car on Sunday. Your partner's position is that they also want the car on Sunday.
2. Think about the reasons behind your position (2–3 reasons you want the car on Sunday) and jot them down on your piece of paper. These reasons are your interests. Since this is a hypothetical problem, feel free to embellish! Do not share your interests until step 3. (Example: One of your interests is that you need to give your mother a ride to the grocery store.)
3. Take turns asking each other about your interests.
4. Determine if there is any possible way that both of your sets of interests can be met. If so, what does this solution look like?

Post-activity discussion questions:

1. How many pairs were able to come to an agreement?
2. For those pairs that were not able to come to an agreement:

   a What was the obstacle?
   b What might have made your tasks easier?

3. For those pairs that were able to negotiate an agreement:

   a What were the specifics of your agreement?
   b What helped you reach the agreement?

4. How could you use this activity during an actual group project?

Take-away: If you only argue your positions, you will often not be able to come to an agreement. Arguing for the reasons (or interests) underlying those positions gives you the opportunity to discover creative solutions to many disagreements.

7.6.2 Visioning activity

This activity helps group members re-energize and refocus. It can be done online or in person.

Object: Develop a newspaper headline or award that depicts the successful conclusion of your project and share this with the group.

Activity:

1. Each team member individually imagines what success on the current project would look like and then create a newspaper headline or an award to reflect that success. Take about ten minutes to develop one or both of these ideas. (Example: "Customers are re-engaged through cutting-edge kiosks that recognize them and call them by name!")
2. Team members share their headlines and/or award descriptions with each other.

Post-activity discussion questions:

1. What was easy, and what was difficult about this activity?
2. How does this activity make you think about the goal(s) of your group? Has it positively impacted your attitude?
3. What can your team do to sustain the energy from this activity?

Take-away: Visioning activities such as this can give you and your teammates perspective. They help you realize that the obstacles with which the group struggles do not have to derail your project, and the end result of your work could be phenomenal.

References

Cahn, D. D., & Abigail, R. A. (2014). *Managing conflict through communication*. Pearson.

Davey, L. (2019). Let your team have that heated conversation. *Harvard Business Review*, December 23. https://hbr.org/2019/12/let-your-team-have-that-heated-conversation.

Epstein, A. (2018). Build self-awareness with help from your team. *Harvard Business Review*, August 13. https://hbr.org/2018/08/build-self-awareness-with-help-from-your-team.

Nawaz. S. (2019). What to do after an uncomfortable conversation with a coworker. *Harvard Business Review*, May 1. https://hbr.org/2019/05/what-to-do-after-an-uncomfortable-conversation-with-a-coworker.

Tuckman, B. W. (1965). Developmental sequence in small groups. *Psychological Bulletin*, 63, 384–399.

Turkle, S. (2016). *Reclaiming conversation: The power of talk in the digital age*. Penguin.

8

DEVELOPING SELF-AWARENESS

Questions to consider

- What are some practices for developing self-awareness?
- What targeted questions can you ask yourself to help you reflect?
- Why is it important to be aware of your strengths and weaknesses?
- What are the benefits and limitations of personality inventories?
- Why is it important to seek out criticism about your group behaviors?

8.1 Introduction

To this point, we have looked at seven practices that will help you become a stronger group member. Any group member will benefit from ascribing to these practices. But, being a good group member is also the result of knowing what specific assets and liabilities you (and others) bring to the group. Before you can pinpoint your specific assets and liabilities to a team, you need to learn about yourself or engage in self-awareness. Self awareness is the extent to which you know yourself.

Randy Fujishin, a speech communication professor and the author of *Creating Effective Groups: The Art of Small Group Communication*, advises that "Before you can really be open to the ideas, opinions, and feelings of others, you must first be open to your own ideas, opinions, and feelings" (Fujishin, 2013, p. 20). Having self-awareness not only makes you a stronger team member, but it also makes the team function at a higher level. In fact, recent management research (Dierdorff, Fisher, & Rubin, 2019) found that there is a direct correlation between teams composed of individuals with greater levels of self-awareness and more effective team-level functioning and performance. Another study shows that leaders who

DOI: 10.4324/9781003285571-9

develop a deep sense of self-awareness by constantly evaluating their own beliefs and values are more effective at leading others (Caldwell & Hayes, 2016). Even if you are not the official group leader, your sense of self-awareness can have a positive impact on your group members.

An easy way to think about self-awareness is to use the Johari Window model. The Johari Window model, developed by American psychologists Joseph Luft and Harry Ingham in 1955, is a method used to understand and enhance communication between group members (Communication Theory, n.d.). The name "Johari" is a combination of the first names of the two men. The Johari Window resembles a windowpane, with intersecting lines creating four quadrants. Each quadrant represents the various types of self-awareness of an individual. The four quadrants are the open self, the blind spot, the hidden self, and the unknown self (see Figure 8.1).

As Figure 8.1 shows, the two left quadrants are the things we know about ourselves. This includes the open self quadrant, and the hidden self quadrant. The open self is the information that we know about ourselves and that we share with others. For instance, I may belong to a band, and I talk about it on a regular basis, so you also know that I am in a band. The hidden self is the information that we know about ourselves but that we choose not to share with others. For instance, one of your group members might be a spy, but they certainly wouldn't let you know that. Two right quadrants of the Johari Window are things we do not know about ourselves. The blind spot is information we do not know about ourselves but others do know about us. For instance, my group members might have made the observation that I frown when I am deep in thought, but until someone tells me, it remains part of my blind spot. The unknown spot is information that neither I nor others know about me. Perhaps I have a-yet-to-surface allergy to down. Until I start sneezing and figure out the allergy, it remains part of the unknown self.

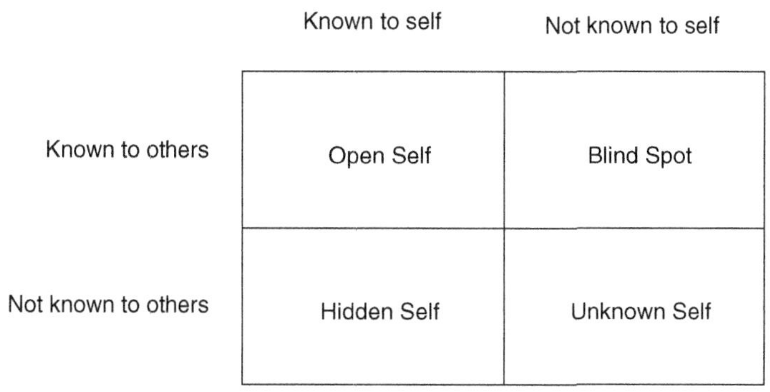

	Known to self	Not known to self
Known to others	Open Self	Blind Spot
Not known to others	Hidden Self	Unknown Self

FIGURE 8.1 The four quadrants of the Johari Window

Knowing that we have different types of self-awareness, can help us to be more amenable to the idea that there are things we don't know about ourselves (blind spots) and that others can help us with these. It also reminds us that we might have strengths that we are not yet aware of.

You will have the opportunity to work further with the concept of the Johari Window at the end of the chapter.

8.2 Practices for developing self-awareness

There are several ways to learn about yourself. Some of the most popular are engaging in reflection, completing personality inventories, asking others for feedback, and engaging in social comparison.

8.2.1 Reflect on yourself

One way to develop self-awareness is to reflect on yourself. Reflecting on yourself is the process of understanding yourself and includes identifying your patterns of thought and behavior and making note of your strengths and opportunities for improvement. Research has shown that self-reflection can improve academic performance (Lew & Schmidt, 2011; Menekse, 2020; Nilson, 2013) as well as boost workplace productivity. In a *Harvard Business Review* article, Porter (2017) explains that "Reflection gives the brain an opportunity to pause amidst the chaos, untangle and sort through observations and experiences, consider multiple possible interpretations, and create meaning."

There are several ways to reflect on yourself: The key is to be intentional. One way to reflect on yourself is to make a list of your strengths, your motivations, and your opportunities for improvement. You could also reflect on yourself in a specific context by thinking about what you learned from this situation. For instance, in our classrooms, we often ask students to reflect at the end of the class by completing a one-minute questionnaire with these questions (as suggested by Angelo & Cross, 1993): "What was the most important thing you learned today?" and "what questions do you still have?" These questions help to reinforce important concepts and encourage students to engage more deeply with class materials.

Similarly, you can engage in this type of self-reflection with teamwork. For example, after a team meeting, think about both your verbal and nonverbal communication, such as the physical positions you may assume during group interactions and the frames of mind you are in. Ask yourself, was that a productive meeting? Was I engaged and contributing? Do I feel my voice was heard? Did I appreciate my teammates' positions? Our recommendation is to set aside some time prior to or after a group meeting to reflect on how you want to (or did, respectively) interact with your group members.

Self reflection can help both your individual performance and the performance of your group. In a workplace study, researchers found that employees who spent

15 minutes at the end of the day reflecting about their training day performed better than those who did not (Di Stefano, Gino, Pisano, & Staats, 2016). Similarly, in the context of teamwork, formal reflection assignments were found to improve self-awareness and team experience in interprofessional and inter-disciplinary teams (McNaughton, 2015; Van Winkle et al., 2013).

The following section details the three targeted questions that we ask group members to consider for themselves.

8.2.1.1 Ask yourself, "What are my typical group behaviors?"

This is probably not the first group you have been in. Reflecting on your past group experiences can be helpful when you join a new group. Often, we tend to assume the same behaviors across groups. Within our groups, we can become known for being timely (or late), active (or absent), realistic (or optimistic), verbose (or reticent), or any number of other adjectives. Ask yourself if you have any typical behaviors when you are in groups and whether these behaviors are generally helpful or disruptive. Chapter 9 explains a form you can fill out to identify and share this information with your team. This form can be found in Appendix B.

Part of assessing your own group behaviors is to identify actions you typically take that help your group be successful. Perhaps you are adept at seeing the big picture, meaning you have a clear idea of how your group's project fits within the larger context of the class or the company. Or, maybe you are good at seeing the interconnected nature of the tasks group members are undertaking or building the morale of the team. Once you know your strengths, you can purposefully use them when they might benefit the group.

Assessing your own group behavior also includes identifying your potential problematic behaviors. Common problematic group behaviors we have observed include taking things personally, responding pessimistically to the ideas of others, trying to push through ideas, and not offering any feedback on the ideas of others. If you exhibit these behaviors, ask yourself if and under what circumstances these actions might be effective.

It is important to beware that your strengths may also be your limitations. The fact that you are extremely organized might make it easy for you to find information related to the project timeline. The fact that you are extremely organized also might indicate you do not handle ambiguity well. Another example of someone's strength being their weakness is the person who is detail-oriented. This person's precision and attention to details might make for an excellent copy editor, but these same skills may be a challenge if the individual is promoted to manager. Being an effective manager requires a totally different skill set - one that requires more coaching and less copyediting. Some new (and not-so-new) managers micromanage their staff. That is, they become overly involved in the day-to-day minutia of their subordinate's tasks. People who micromanage their staff are typically those who have difficulty giving up control of some product or process.

8.2.1.2 Ask yourself, "What are my typical frustrations with groups?"

People also tend to have individual frustrations that recur when they are working in groups. Perhaps you are predisposed to action and you become frustrated with long discussions where decisions are not being made quickly enough to suit you. Alternatively, perhaps you like to consider various angles to an issue before you make a decision. Group members who want to immediately jump to action may irritate you (see Appendix B for a list of group behaviors that may be frustrating to you). It is important that you recognize what frustrates you or what triggers your negative emotions. This recognition or mindfulness allows you to take steps to face the situation or to mitigate your feelings.

As we discuss in Chapter 9, the best way to avoid these frustrations with groups is to have a candid conversation and a team contract at the beginning of your team project so that everyone is on the same page, not just regarding the project itself, but also in terms of everyone's expectations with group behaviors. However, sometimes, you may end up on a team midway through the project, when that conversation or meeting has already passed. In this case, it is important for you to articulate your concerns with the group.

Some concerns are fairly easy to address with your group. For instance, when your frustrations or concerns deal with a group process, group members are unlikely to take your criticism personally. If you recognize that some of your teammates are not communicating on the agreed-upon Slack channel or instant message app, you could voice this concern at the next group meeting. During the conversation, you could try to determine what (if any) miscommunication happened or what (if any) problems members are having with using the medium. If neither is the case, you could emphasize the importance of all members using the same platform to communicate so that no one misses any messages.

Other concerns may be more difficult to address. If you are experiencing excessive frustrations, consider how these frustrations might be contributing to your overall stress or negatively impacting your work. As Cross, Singer, and Dillon (2020) describe, "Stress comes to us all in tiny little assaults throughout our day." These, "micro-stresses," they explain, take a toll on our health and productivity. If recurrent or more serious frustrations are draining your energy or impacting your ability to complete your work, it is important to try to find a way to talk with your group members about what is frustrating you. Refer back to Chapter 5 for ways to present and explore ideas. If the conversation could become charged, refer back to Chapter 7 to review effective practices for providing and accepting constructive feedback.

8.2.1.3 Ask yourself, "How do I think this group could run better?"

Self-awareness can be extended to group awareness. Just as it is important for you to understand yourself, your motivations, your strengths, your frustrators, your opportunities for improvement, it is important to have an understanding of your group. If the dynamics in your group are shifting or problematic, you want to be aware of this. Sometimes, groups hit points of impasse or maybe they never quite gained traction. This can happen for several reasons, and sometimes the group remains stuck for a while. But oftentimes, there is one or more group members who sees what the issue is. If they called this issue to the attention of the group, the group might be able to rectify it. But if they remain silent, the group may carry on in dysfunctional processes.

One of our colleagues was part of a group that had two changes in leadership within a five-month period because during that five months, the group had accomplished nothing. The meetings went round in circles, with the same group members reiterating their specific concerns, and no forward progress was ever made. Our colleague sat silently in these meetings with plenty of ideas to move forward, but she simply didn't have the confidence to speak up. When she talked with us about the meetings, she concluded, "Nothing is ever decided. We keep rehashing the same issues." This group was experiencing analysis paralysis. Our advice to our colleague was to speak up in a meeting and suggest that certain issues be put to a vote so that the group could move on. It was quite simple advice, provided by our colleague herself. However, it took us giving her permission to make this suggestion before she had the confidence to do so.

If you are a member of a group that doesn't seem to be making any traction, there are a couple of actions you can take. We recommend that you first talk with the group leader or facilitator (if there is one) and forewarn them that you are going to make a suggestion to the team at the next meeting. In the case of our example, you might tell the group facilitator, "I have an idea for how to make our meetings more productive. It involves taking periodic votes with the team, and I'd like to explain this at tomorrow's meeting. Do you have any concerns with this?" If your group is less formal or you do not have a leader, you can simply bring the idea up with the entire group at the beginning or end of the next meeting. In fact, some groups struggle precisely because there is no leadership in the group. If your group has no leader, you may need to adjust your own behaviors to take on some of the roles of a leader, including asking difficult questions of the group and keeping the conversation on track. See Chapter 9 for more suggestions.

8.2.2 Take personality inventories

Another way to develop self-awareness is to take personality inventories or tests that might provide you insight into yourself. There are several paid personality inventories commonly used in the workplace including DISC, Myers–Briggs Type Indicator, and 16 Personality Factor Questionnaire:

- DISC is a "non-judgmental personality and behavioral assessment used by more than one million people every year to improve teamwork, communication, and productivity" (DISC, n.d.).
- The Myers–Briggs Type Indicator (MBTI) identifies "16 distinctive personality types… allowing you to approach your own work in a manner that best suits your style" (Myers–Briggs Foundation, n.d.).
- 16 Personality Factor Questionnaire (commonly known as "16PF Questionnaire") is used to measure "16 different primary personality characteristics structured around the 'Big Five' global factors of personality" (16PF, n.d.).

When you are trying to develop your self-awareness, such inventories can be a good place to start. They might help you articulate your inclinations, tendencies, antipathies, and picallos.

Other, shorter, inventories, such as the "Which Shape Are You?" activity (found in Appendix A) can be useful in starting to think about your strengths, weaknesses, and preferences when it comes to working in a group. Fujishin (2013) offers several simple inventories to help the reader discover things about themself. One of these is titled "Your Communication Behaviors" (p. 25), which asks you to indicate whether we strongly disagree, disagree, unsure, agree, or strongly agree with a series of statements. Following is an excerpt from this inventory. These particular statements are targeted at your verbal and nonverbal communication behaviors.

For each of these statements, select whether you strongly disagree (1), disagree (2), are unsure (3), agree (4), or strongly agree (5).

1. I speak in a pleasant tone of voice.
2. I speak at an adequate rate (speed) of speech.
3. I have a relaxed posture when speaking.
4. I use expressive gestures when speaking.
5. I smile when I speak with others.
6. I make eye contact when speaking with others.
7. I nod my head in agreement when listening.

These statements correspond to verbal and nonverbal behaviors that are typically considered desirable in group interactions. For this reason, if you assigned yourself a 1 or 2 to any statement, you may want to adjust your behavior accordingly.

Regardless of the particular inventory you use, know that the results are only a snapshot in time, a static result of one's dynamic personality. Additionally, all inventories are limited in their design, so beware of anything that is too authoritarian about who you are and how you should behave. At best, the results of such tests should only be used as one more piece of information input to your decisions.

Self-reflections, whether structured (through an inventory) or unstructured, are a good way to begin developing self-awareness, However, as the Johari Window suggests, there are parts of ourselves that we are not aware of. Hence, we can only learn so much through reflection alone. Another way to gain self-awareness is to ask others for feedback.

8.2.3 Ask others for feedback

People's initial reaction might be to avoid criticism, and we find that students are often hesitant in honestly evaluating their peers' performance. However, feedback alerts us to potential blind spots and provides us with ideas for modifying our behavior. Refer back to Chapter 2 for tips on providing targeted feedback.

Seeking feedback is found to have a positive impact at work. In one study, researchers found that feedback-seeking from team members could be conducive to thriving at work, thus promoting their creativity. Therefore, they recommend establishing "feedback-seeking climates" at work to encourage employees to seek feedback from team members (Wang, Wang, & Liu, 2021). Feedback can also be used in conjunction with reflection. One study shows that reflective journaling that focuses on peer evaluation and feedback can indeed improve teamwork competencies (Hoo, Tan, & Deneen, 2020).

Just as it is important to be able to provide constructive feedback, it is important to know how to request it. You could ask a trusted group member or friend how you might be more effective in meetings. Ask them to share their observations and insights with you. You could even ask specific questions, like, "How did my comment about XYZ come off?" or "How could I have better reacted to Aiden's criticism?"

While it is typically more common to ask for constructive feedback to improve ourselves, we should also ask for positive feedback to validate our abilities and contributions. Research shows that positive feedback is equally important in validating our behaviors. For example, researchers found that validating positive emotions at work leads to "improved relationship quality and trust, as well as increased positivity and well-being that can result in enhanced learning behavior and collaboration" (Paakkanen, Martela, & Pessi, 2021, p. 1). You could ask a trusted teammate, "What do you see as my strengths on this team?" or "What should I continue to do in group meetings?"

8.2.4 Engage in social comparison

Engaging in social comparison is another way to develop or increase your self-awareness. Social comparison is looking to others who are similar to us in some way and measuring our abilities or behaviors against theirs. For instance, if I am new to playing piano, I might compare my progress to that of another novice pianist. The result of this comparison may be that I decide I'm not a very good pianist. Another example of social comparison would be using my peers as a gauge for how I am participating in a group. I could ask myself questions such as "Do I seem as committed as my teammates?" and "How do my persuasion skills stack up against those of my teammates?" The result of these comparisons could be my awareness that I am a solid contributor but less persuasive as other members.

The purpose of social comparisons is not to give you an ego boost (because you are more talented than someone else) or to make yourself feel bad (because you aren't as effective or as successful as someone else). Rather, it is to gain an understanding of where you are now and what work you need to do to improve.

Workplace researchers found that employees who receive feedback about their coworkers' contributions tend to contribute more to group work than when they do not receive such feedback (Chen, Zhang, & Latimer, 2014). In another study, the researchers found that how employees engage in social comparisons could impact their work. More specifically, "making unrealistic or inappropriate comparisons may damage one's sense of self-worth, whereas making accurate, relevant comparisons may ensure that one's work meets managerial or organizational expectations" (Margolis & Dust, 2019, p. 380).

Social comparisons can also help you make decisions about how to act in a specific situation, particularly in a situation that is unfamiliar to you. When Tammy was a first-time manager, she often found herself pondering the question, "What would Craig do?" Craig was a boss Tammy had many years ago. Craig was very effective and well-respected by his employees. By asking herself what Craig might do in a similar situation, Tammy was able to devise a specific course of action that she believed an effective boss would take.

Think about previous teams you have worked on. Is there any particular member who stands out in your memory as being a good group member? If yes, then ask yourself what characteristics made them so great. Do you share those characteristics with them? Is that why you appreciate it so much? Or, do you wish you had that characteristic? Your answers to these questions should give you some insight into who you are and how others might perceive you. When you think about your previous teams, also consider the types of teammates you have not appreciated so much. What did you dislike about working with them? You will probably come up with some tangible characteristics of someone you considered a bad group member. Once you share any of these characteristics? How might others react to these characteristics?

8.4 Putting self-awareness into action

Once you have done some self-reflection, perhaps talked with others, and possibly taken a personality inventory, you should have a good level of self-awareness. You can use this knowledge about yourself to refine your group interactions.

More specifically, once you are aware of your own behaviors, you can adjust your behaviors or use them more purposefully.

Let's look at an example. Perhaps you have a tendency to interrupt others. In whatever way you discover this fact about yourself (whether it was through reflection, or talking to others, or taking a personality-inventory) you might catch yourself when you start to interrupt someone in the future. Realizing that interruption is not a favorable trait, you might be more apt to attempt to interrupt others less often. In this sense, self-awareness prompts you to adjust your behavior and take action (or in this case, inaction) that you might not otherwise have taken.

Your self-awareness can impact the decisions and the work of your group. For instance, let's say that you tend to avoid conflict and typically just go along with whatever the group decides. But at one group meeting, you are certain that the group is making a poor decision. Knowing that you tend to avoid conflict, but also realizing that an issue needs to be raised, you might decide to push yourself to tell the group, "I have some concerns about this decision."

Self-awareness in groups also allows you to act purposefully with your group members. For example, let's say that you are not a particularly critical person. This knowledge about yourself may not also include the desire to change, but you could use that knowledge to call on the strengths of other group members. Asking something like, "What are we not looking at with this solution?" allows you to ask for others to be critical of the current idea. This is an effective technique, particularly if you are very attached to an idea but want to make you are considering all aspects of a solution.

Putting your self-awareness into action will help you to be a more effective team member.

8.5 Summary

This chapter explains the following key points about developing self-awareness:

- Reflect on yourself to develop a greater sense of self-awareness.
- Ask yourself what your typical group behaviors are, what your typical group frustrations are, and how you think your group can improve.
- Take personality inventories to identify your strengths, abilities, and preferences.
- Be proactive by asking others for both positive and constructive feedback.
- Engage in social comparison to motivate yourself and improve your contributions to the team.
- Use your knowledge about yourself to refine your group interactions.

8.6 Discussion questions

1. When was the last time that you reflected on your strengths, weaknesses, and/or preferences?

2. Do you journal or write down your thoughts or experiences? If so, what benefits does it provide you?
3. Have you ever taken a personality inventory? If so, what did you think of the results? How did they impact your behaviors?
4. Have you ever given feedback to someone about their group behavior? If so, how did it go? If not, can you think of a situation where it might have been helpful?
5. Can you think of a time you used social comparisons to help you make a decision about how to act in a specific situation? What was the result?

8.7 Activities

8.7.1 Moodboard revisited

This is an individual activity that can be done in both online and in-person settings.

Object: This activity asks individuals to reflect on their own moodboards.

Activity: Take a look at the moodboard you created for Chapter 4. Ask yourself the following questions about your own moodboard:

1. What do these images suggest about me? Choose three descriptive words or phrases (For instance, *adventurous, eclectic,* and *animal-lover*)
2. What images would I *not* consider adding to this mood board? (For instance, a *messy room, totaled car,* and *blackjack table*). Do any of these images correspond with aspects of my hidden self?
3. In five years, what images would I like to be able to add to my moodboard? What do they suggest about my aspirations and personality traits?

Take-away: Besides being a tool for sharing with others, the moodboard can help us develop our own self-awareness.

8.7.2 Johari Window

This activity works best in-person.

Object: This activity helps the individual work with the concept of the Johari Window by using self-reflection and feedback provided by group members.

Setup: Before the activity begins, each group member should have 2–3 blank pieces of paper and a pencil.

Activity:

Part I Providing feedback.

1. Divide the first sheet of paper into four smaller pieces. At the top of each of the smaller papers, write the name of one group member. Be

sure to write your own name at the top of one of the papers. If you have more than four group members, you will need to use an additional sheet of paper.

2. Write down two words or phrases that describe that group member on each group member's page (including your own). **Example**: *friendly* and *likes to stand during meetings*

3. Fold the papers and provide them to the appropriate group members.

Part II Creating the Johari Window.

1. Create four quadrants by drawing a horizontal line and a vertical line that intersect on the second sheet of paper. In the upper left quadrant, write, "Open Self," and in the upper right quadrant, write, "Blind Spot." In the lower left quadrant, write, "Hidden Self," and in the lower right quadrant, write, "Unknown Self." Use Figure 8.1 as a guide.

2. Open the folded papers provided to you by your group members and copy the words and phrases onto one of the quadrants of your Johari Window. If you agree with the word, write it in the *Open Self* quadrant. If you are surprised by the word (or initially disagree with it), write it in the *Blind Spot* quadrant. (Later, you can decide if it truly is a blind spot, or if it is something else). At this point, you should only have words in the "Open Self" and (perhaps) "Blind Spot" quadrants.

3. Think about any thoughts, traits, and behaviors that you have not shared with your group or that they have not discovered. **Examples**: *Punctual. Impatient with people who complain at length.* You could add these words and phrases to the *Hidden Self* quadrant (but you don't need to).

4. If you completed the "Moodboard revisited" activity (section 8.7.1 above), look back to your response to question 3. Ask yourself, "Could any of the images that I would like to add to my moodboard indicate my *Unknown Self?*"

Part III Discussion.

• Discuss with your group members what (if anything) you learned about yourself from their feedback. Also discuss your responses to Question 4 (regarding the *Unknown Self*).

Take-away: The Johari Window is a helpful tool for thinking about our own levels of self-awareness.

References

16PF. (n.d.). Key benefits. Retrieved August 11, 2022, from www.16pf.com/en_US/16pf-overview/key-benefits.

Angelo, T. A., & Cross, K. P. (1993). *Classroom assessment techniques: A handbook for college teachers*, 2nd edition. Jossey-Bass.

Caldwell, C., & Hayes, L. A. (2016). Self-efficacy and self-awareness: Moral insights to increased leader effectiveness. *Journal of Management Development*, 35(9), 1163–1173. https:// doi.org/10.1108/JMD-01-2016-0011.

Chen, F., Zhang, L., & Latimer, J. (2014). How much has my co-worker contributed? The impact of anonymity and feedback on social loafing in asynchronous virtual collaboration. *International Journal of Information Management*, 34(5), 652–659. https://doi.org/ 10.1016/j.ijinfomgt.2014.05.001.

Communication Theory. (n.d.). The Johari Window model. Retrieved August 7, 2022, from www.communicationtheory.org/the-johari-window-model/.

Cross, R., Singer, J., & Dillon, K. (2020). Don't let micro-stresses burn you out. *Harvard Business Review*, July 9. https://hbr.org/2020/07/dont-let-micro-stresses-burn-you-out.

Dierdorff, E. C., Fisher, D. M., & Rubin, R. S. (2019). The power of percipience: Consequences of self-awareness in teams on team-level functioning and performance. *Journal of Management, 45(7), 2891–2919.* https://doi.org/10.1177/0149206318774622.

DISC. (n.d.). DISC profile. www.discprofile.com/.

Di Stefano, G., Gino, F., Pisano, G. P., & Staats, B. R. (2016). *Making experience count: The role of reflection in individual learning.* IDEAS Working Paper Series from RePEc. https:// doi.org/10.2139/ssrn.2874177.

Fujishin, R. (2013). *Creating effective groups: The art of small group communication.* Rowman & Littlefield Publishers.

Hoo, H., Tan, K., & Deneen, C. (2020). Negotiating self- and peer-feedback with the use of reflective journals: An analysis of undergraduates' engagement with feedback. *Assessment and Evaluation in Higher Education*, 45(3), 431–446. https://doi.org/10.1080/ 02602938.2019.1665166.

Lew, M. D. N., & Schmidt, H. G. (2011). Self-reflection and academic performance: Is there a relationship? *Advances in Health Sciences Education: Theory and Practice*, 16(4), 529–545. https://doi.org/10.1007/s10459-011-9298-z.

Margolis, J. A., & Dust, S. B. (2019). It's all relative: A team-based social comparison model for self-evaluations of effectiveness. *Group & Organization Management*, 44(2), 361–395. https://doi.org/10.1177/1059601116682901.

McNaughton. S. M. (2015). Students' reflections on first-year interprofessional teamwork: Phenomenographic evaluation of function and success. *Focus on Health Professional Education*, 16(3), 86–100. https://doi.org/10.11157/fohpe.v16i3.82.

Menekse, M. (2020). The reflection-informed learning and instruction to improve students' academic success in undergraduate classrooms. *The Journal of Experimental Education, 88(2), 183–199.* https://doi.org/10.1080/00220973.2019.1620159.

Myers–Briggs Foundation. (n.d.). MBTI basics. www.myersbriggs.org/my-mbti-personality-type/mbti-basics/.

Nilson, L. B. (2013). *Creating self-regulated learners: Strategies to strengthen self-awareness and learning skills.* Stylus Publishing.

Paakkanen, M. A., Martela, F., & Pessi, A. B. (2021). Responding to positive emotions at work – the four steps and potential benefits of a validating response to coworkers' positive experiences. *Frontiers in Psychology*, 12, 668160–668160. https://doi.org/10. 3389/fpsyg.2021.668160.

Porter, J. (2017). Why you should make time for self-reflection (even if you hate doing it). *Harvard Business Review*, March 21. https://hbr.org/2017/03/why-you-should-make-time-for-self-reflection-even-if-you-hate-doing-it.

Van Winkle, L. J., Cornell, S., Fjortoft, N., Bjork, B. C., Chandar, N., Green, J. M., La Salle, S., Viselli, S. M., Burdick, P., & Lynch, S. M. (2013). Critical thinking and reflection exercises in a biochemistry course to improve prospective health professions students' attitudes toward physician-pharmacist collaboration. *American Journal of Pharmaceutical Education*, 77(8), 169–169. https://doi.org/10.5688/ajpe778169.

Wang, T., Wang, D., & Liu, Z. (2021). Feedback-seeking from team members increases employee creativity: The roles of thriving at work and mindfulness. *Asia Pacific Journal of Management*. https://doi.org/10.1007/s10490-021-09768-8.

9

MAKING YOUR MEETINGS PRODUCTIVE

Questions to consider

- What are the benefits of having a team contract?
- What items are typically included on a meeting agenda?
- What are the three common meeting roles?
- Why is it important to predetermine as a group how decisions should be made?
- What is the best way to close a meeting?

9.1 Introduction to documents and processes

In addition to developing your interpersonal skills, you can help your groups be effective by using documents and processes to accomplish the work of the team. The particulars of documents and processes depend on the group. Some groups are more formal than others, and as such, will religiously refer to specific documents and follow with aplomb time-honored practices. Many organizations and committees follow Robert's Rules of Order because it provides an orderly and consistent way of conducting meetings and making decisions.

For instance, we both regularly attend meetings where a member of the meeting must make a motion and a second member second that motion to commence the process of accepting the latest meeting minutes. All of this formality to say: *Yes; we do all accept the assertions of the document that states what was stated the last time we spoke!*

But we have also been part of groups that used neither documents nor (apparent) processes. Inevitably, these meetings can end up feeling like a big "rap" session where no one has any idea what they are supposed to do next

DOI: 10.4324/9781003285571-10

or why. This is not only frustrating but also devastating to team success. One study (Kauffeld & Lehmann-Willenbrock, 2012) found that better team meetings not only led to higher team productivity, but also contributed to constructive team interaction and organizational success. Therefore, it is important to have both documents and processes that can ensure productive meetings.

Our position is that even the most informal team can benefit from a few basic documents and processes. The documents and processes on the following pages are not intended to be a comprehensive accounting of helpful meeting ideas. Rather, they represent what we have seen as the most common in the various groups with which we have engaged. We begin by presenting the three basic documents that every team needs. Next, we offer three critical processes that will help your team thrive.

9.2 Helpful documents

To set your team up for success, your group will want to create and maintain a few documents to help keep the team on track and to document such information as the scope of the project, team tasks and roles, budget (if applicable), timelines, and progress. The documents that cover these areas are the team contract, project plan, and meeting agenda.

9.2.1 Team contract

As we mention in the "Introduction," chances are that your team will be diverse, with members having various viewpoints. For this reason, it is important for everyone to be on the same page from the start of the team project. Students often have a tendency to shy away from the "hard questions" if they don't know each other well. For example, they may be hesitant to discuss how to handle conflicts or disagreements or what is reasonable (or unreasonable) when it comes to response time or quality of work. This contract-writing process allows those conversations to happen before the team members are faced with these types of incidents.

A team contract documents expectations of group members and "operating procedures" for the group. For instance, a team contract might indicate that members are responsible for attending weekly in-person or online meetings, maintaining a respectful team atmosphere, and completing their individual tasks in a timely manner. A team contract is typically discussed and signed at the beginning of a project. All group members need to sign the contract for it to be considered valid. While it is not a legal document, it is a document the team can refer to in the future if anyone has questions about what they agreed to or if group members are perceived as somehow breaking the contract.

Team contracts are typically used in the classroom setting, but we have found that they can work equally as well in some workplaces. Your team contract may be as specific or as general as your group feels necessary. One aspect of the contract might specify how the group will make decisions in the event that you are at an impasse.

Figure 9.1 shows a simple team contract that we have used in collaborative writing groups. You will notice that in addition to the standard agreement we provide (as instructors), groups may indicate additional requirements or even sanctions that the group will take in the event that a team member "breaks" the contract.

For instance, if your team uses this simple format, you may decide as a group to define such terms as "reasonable amount of time" or what constitutes "quality" work. The following questions will help your group determine what information

Project Contract

Project name (topic): _____

Date: _____

We, the undersigned, agree that the project which we are undertaking requires dedicated collaboration. We will adhere to the task assignments and deadlines determined by our group and set forth in the project plan.

Failure to attend group planning sessions, complete quality assigned work by agreed-upon deadlines or communicate in a reasonable period of time will result in penalties up to and including expulsion from the group and failure of the course.

Additional group expectations:

_____

_____

_____

_____

Signatures:

_____

_____

_____

_____

FIGURE 9.1 Simple team contract

should be added to the "Additional Group Expectations" section of the simple team contract:

- **Communication/Engagement:** What is the expected response time for emails, texts, or online chat? What will you do if a member does not engage or communicate actively (as defined by the contract) in discussions regarding the project?
- **Attendance:** If you plan to meet outside of class to work on the project, how many absences or tardies are allowed? How much prior notification should be given for late/missed meetings? How much time does the team member have to "make up" for missed work?
- **Quality of work:** How should you address the team member who fails to meet expectations for the assignment or hands in shoddy work? How should the member be warned or notified?
- **Deadlines:** How should you address the team member who fails to share or submit his/her work on time? How should the person be warned or notified?
- **Termination:** Under what circumstances should a member be "fired" from the team?

In our experience, the questions above are related to issues that commonly arise in teamwork, so it is important for the team to develop honest expectations, policies, and procedures before they start working together to ensure optimal collaboration.

9.2.2 Basic project plan

A basic project plan is a document that lays out specific tasks necessary to complete the project and the date by which each of the tasks needs to be completed. The project plan also identifies which (if any) of those tasks are contingent upon other tasks and who is responsible for the completion of each task. Project plans help the group keep track of work that has been completed, work that is in-progress, and work that still needs to be completed.

Project plans can also help avoid "unexpected" surprises in the project. As the author of *Team Writing: A Guide to Working in Groups,* Joanna Wolfe (2010) explains, team members often have different work styles and expectations, and if they don't clearly understand their responsibilities and the deadlines, conflict can occur at critical points of the project. The project plan helps everyone on the team be clear on what needs to happen and when.

An easy way to create a project plan is to use a simple Gantt chart, like the one shown in Figure 9.2. The tasks that make up the project and the team member responsible for each of these tasks are listed down the left side of the chart. On the top of the chart, the dates are broken out by weeks. The bars across the chart indicate which tasks need to be completed by which dates. As you can see in this

Project Plan: Preconstruction for Pedestrian Bridge

ACTIVITY	RESPONSIBLE	PERCENT COMPLETE	MAY					JUNE	
			May 1	May 8	May 15	May 22	May 29	June 5	June 12
Erosian control	Ravi	100%							
Temp fencing	Lily	100%							
Temp signage	Graham	35%							
Install signal lights	Lily	0%							
Temp pavement	Graham	0%							
Reroute eastbound	Ravi	0%							
First precast	Shanae	0%							

FIGURE 9.2 Sample project plan

example, some tasks can be completed **concurrently** (at the same time). However, some tasks are contingent (dependent) on the completions of other tasks.

Some teams include project plan information in their contracts, but we prefer to separate the two because, while project plans can and do change, the contract typically does not.

It is important to know that the project plan is a guide, not a dictate. It is a living and breathing document, meaning that you will be continually revising and updating your project plan to reflect what is happening on your project. If, for instance, one task on the plan is unable to be completed (due to lack of resources or another reason), it is likely that other, contingent tasks will also be delayed. The project plan should be updated to reflect these types of situations.

In some teams, you will have a project manager. If you have a project manager on your team, that person is responsible for creating and updating the project plan. Even if your team does not have a project manager, you could suggest that your team create (and regularly update) a project plan to keep everyone aware of how their work interacts with the work of others in the group.

Your project plan may need to be updated for a number of reasons (e.g., unexpected delays in task completion, sudden lack of necessary resources, or team conflicts), which is why we recommend that you incorporate progress reports into your project plan. The progress report does not necessarily need to be a formal document, but it prompts you to answer these three "what" questions: What have you accomplished? What are you working on now? And what do you still have to do to complete the project? This is also a good time to do an "energy" checkup with your team. As we mentioned in Chapter 7, it is important to refocus your team if you have experienced major conflicts or disagreements that affected your team's energy level or morale.

9.2.3 Meeting agenda

Robert's Rules of Order requires each meeting to have an agenda so that all members are aware of the discussion items (Robert et al., 2020). Think of a meeting agenda as a conversational plan that will ensure a fair give and take. It lays out the topics and the order in which they will be discussed in a meeting. Some groups use agendas and others do not. In general, the more formal the meeting, the more likely it is that that team will have a meeting agenda.

A basic agenda lists the topics that will be discussed at the meeting. Sometimes this is separated into old and new business. Old business includes topics that have previously been discussed but need further attention. New business includes new topics that will be covered in the current meeting. Sometimes, agendas also indicate the person who is responsible for managing the particular topics being discussed. See Figure 9.3 for a sample agenda.

Agendas are also an attempt to keep conversation focused and the group effective. According to the author of the *Surprising Science of Meetings* Dr. Stephen Rogelberg (2019) found that only 50% of meetings are effective, and there is a strong correlation between job satisfaction and meeting experience. Furthermore, in a survey of meeting participants (Leach et al., 2009), the result shows that distributing a written agenda before meetings can lead to perceived meeting effectiveness and a good use of time. Therefore, meeting agendas are your first line of defense against team members **hijacking** the meeting by spending meeting time discussing topics that are off-track.

In our experience, many more workplace teams than classroom teams use agendas. Even if your team does not use agendas, it's important that someone (maybe you!) start the meeting by restating the purpose of the meeting ("As a reminder, our task today is to start programming the robot.") and then asking if anyone has any issues or questions that need to be addressed before you start ("Before we jump in, is there anything else we need to discuss or any questions we need to clarify?"). In this sense, you are addressing the group's "old business" before starting the new.

Meeting Agenda
March 27, 20xx

1. Announcements – All
2. Old Business

   a. Review of Site Map – Daryl
   b. Review of Appendix A (v.3) – Toya

3. New Business

   a. Review of Appendix B (v.2) – Colton
   b. Review of Appendix C (v.2) – Toya

FIGURE 9.3 Sample agenda

9.3 Important processes

To make the most of your meetings, your team should also work to create an environment that is both productive and safe. See the Introduction of this book for a definition of participative safety. Such an environment will improve the chances that disagreements can be handled openly and directly. We have identified the following additional processes that will help make your meetings productive.

9.3.1 Determine how you will make decisions

When you are working in a group, there will be times when group members do not all agree on a course of action or decision that needs to be made. When the group cannot reach a consensus, it is helpful if the members know how they will negotiate their differences and make a final decision. There are several ways of making decisions. Following are three options that we have used in our groups:

- **Majority rules**. This method works if your team has an uneven number of members, e.g., 3, 5, or 7. You will vote on the issue when there is a disagreement, and the group will go with the decision with the majority vote. If your team has an even number, then this option will not work.
- **Compromise.** In a typical workplace environment, it is not possible to "die on every battle hill," which means compromise is often necessary to help the team move forward. So, it is helpful to ask yourself what your "non-negotiables" are beforehand and share them with your team.
- **Client (or instructor) decides.** If the team works with an external client, then the team can bring the options to the client and ask them to decide which option/method is the best or most ideal. In our experience, the "instructor decides" method should be the last resort where or when there are irreconcilable differences between the team members. As we mention in Chapter 5, it is important for team members to learn how to negotiate their differences instead of putting the onus on the instructor or the manager in the workplace.
- **Paper takes rock (or coin flip).** Although coin flipping or "paper takes rock" may seem illogical or unscientific methods for deciding between two options, Haden (2018), citing research conducted by a neuroscientist and a psychologist, argues that when we are torn between two seemingly equal choices, our brain already knows what the right choice is. For example, if the coin lands on "heads," (or the first option), and you immediately think, "that is the right choice," then you should go ahead with that decision; but, if you think "wait, let's do two out of three," then you already decide (in your brain) that "tails" or the second option is better.

We advise our students and group members to decide on the method they will use to make decisions as part of one of their initial team meetings and to state this in their group contract before any disagreements occur.

9.3.2 Establish meeting roles

In addition to project-related roles (that dictate the type of tasks for which each group member is responsible), there are specific tasks that need to be completed during group meetings. We've divided these tasks into three roles:

- **Meeting facilitator**. This person should manage the structure of the meeting and keep everyone on task. This includes encouraging others to contribute and **tabling** (temporarily putting aside) discussions that are not immediately relevant. Preparing and following the agenda is typically the responsibility of this person.
- **Note-taker/recorder.** This person takes notes that summarize the topics that were covered and the decisions that were made during the meeting. They also capture who is responsible for what, and the deadlines that are agreed-upon. Sometimes the notetaker also prepares **meeting minutes**, which is a document that can then distribute the meeting minutes prior to or at the next meeting. Alternatively, the notetaker can send an email reminder that summarizes to-dos and their responsible team members and due dates.
- **Timekeeper**. At minimum, this person should give a couple of time checks, typically half-way through the meeting and five minutes before the end of the meeting.

Having a role in the meeting allows you to put yourselves in the right mindset when you are in a meeting. For example, as the secretary of a professional organization, Felicia's main role was to take minutes during the executive committee meetings. In this role, she was intentional about asking for clarifications to make sure that the minutes were correctly recorded. Even if you don't have an official role in a meeting, it is important that you are still an active, contributing member.

Although in informal meetings, one person can fulfill several roles, we recommend assigning or rotating different members to these roles. As we discussed in Chapter 2, multitasking may sound like a great idea, but it is actually difficult to do it well.

9.3.3 Close meetings with a plan

Just as you signal you are about to exit from many conversations, your group should also signal that information needs to be exchanged before the meeting comes to a close. For this reason, it's important that you (or another group member) ask the group if there are any additional issues that need to be addressed. Simply asking, "Is there anything else we need to cover or any questions anyone has?" provides group members who are timid or less vocal the opportunity to be heard. Before the meeting is over, it's also a great idea to review what tasks each person needs to complete before the next meeting. If you have a group leader, and they do not address this topic, you could ask the leader, "Could we quickly review who's doing what before our next meeting?"

9.4 Summary

This chapter explains the following key points about the documents, procedures, and process that will help your team's meetings be productive and enjoyable:

- Create a project plan so that every team member can keep track of work that has been completed, work that is in-progress, and work that still needs to be completed.
- Develop a team contract as soon as your team is formed to establish honest and realistic expectations.
- Use a meeting agenda when calling or facilitating a meeting.
- Pre-determine how decisions will be made when there is a disagreement.
- Establish meeting roles, and close meetings with a plan.

9.5 Discussion questions

1. What was your most positive team meeting experience, and why?
2. What do you get most frustrated about when it comes to a team meeting, and why?
3. What information might you want to add to the simple team contract presented in this chapter?
4. What is a meeting role that you are most familiar with (e.g., facilitator, recorder, time-keeper, contributing participant)?
5. How do you prefer to make a decision where there is a disagreement?

9.6 Activities

9.6.1 "Which shape are you?"

This activity is adopted from *Soft skills to pay the bills: Mastering soft skills for workplace success* published by the US Department of Labor (2012). It can be completed either in person or online. The goal of the activity is for all team members to gain a better understanding of the different roles that are necessary for team success.

Object: The object of this activity is for each team member to choose a shape that best represents themself and to explore various interpretations of each shape's "meaning."

Setup: In an in-person setting, prepare five pieces of paper, each with the following shapes drawn: square, rectangle, circle, triangle, and squiggle. In an online setting, share a document with those five shapes drawn on the screen so that everyone can clearly see the shapes.

Activity:

1. Take a couple of minutes to look at each shape and think about the shape you like best or find most appealing.
2. Take turns to share/identify the shape that you choose.
3. Answer the discussion questions below as a group.
4. Read the "key" to the shapes in Appendix A.

Discussion questions:

1. Why did you choose your shape? What did it indicate to you?
2. How much do you agree or disagree with the interpretations of the shapes' meanings that are provided in Appendix A?
3. Why do you think it is important to have all different shapes working on the same team?
4. Why is it important to not only understand how you work best, but to learn how others work best?

Take-away: Team success is dependent on having different types of talents and personalities working together toward a common goal.

9.6.2 Pre-contract questionnaire and discussion

This activity can be done in person or online. In part I of this activity, each team member should complete the pre-contract questionnaire individually. The second part of the activity is for all team members to discuss their answers.

Object: The object of the activity is to give all team members a chance to express how they each approach teamwork and collaboration.

Setup: Print out copies of Appendix B.

Activity:

Part I Each team member should spend 5–7 minutes completing the 9-question Pre-Contract Teamwork Questionnaire (see Appendix B) on their own. It is important to remember that there is no "right" answer for these questions. The goal is to get a better sense of each other's preferences and interests.

Part II The group should reconvene to share their answers.

Take-away: Our past collaboration experience shapes our expectations and approach to teamwork. This activity allows you to examine our own past group behaviors and use this knowledge in a productive way.

References

Haden, J. (2018). How flipping a coin can actually help you make smarter decisions, backed by science. www.inc.com/jeff-haden/how-flipping-a-coin-can-actually-help-you-make-smarter-decisions-backed-by-science.html.

Kauffeld, S. & Lehmann-Willenbrock, N. (2012). Meetings matter: Effects of team meetings on team and organizational success. *Small Group Research*, 43(2), 130–158. https://doi.org/10.1177/1046496411429599.

Leach, D. J., Rogelberg, S. G., Warr, P. B., & Burnfield, J. L. (2009). Perceived meeting effectiveness: The role of design characteristics. *Journal of Business Psychology*, 24(1), 65–76. https://doi.org/10.1007/s10869-009-9092-6.

Robert, H. M., Robert, H. M., Evans, W. J., Honemann, D. H., Balch, T. J., Seabold, D. E., & Gerber, S. (2020). *Robert's Rules of order, newly revised in brief: Updated to accord with the twelfth edition of the complete manual.* PublicAffairs.

Rogelberg, S. G. (2019). *The surprising science of meetings: How you can lead your team to peak performance.* Oxford University Press.

US Department of Labor. (2012). Soft skills to pay the bills: Mastering soft skills for workplace success. www.dol.gov/odep/topics/youth/softskills/.

Wolfe, J. (2010). *Team writing: A guide to working in groups.* Bedford St. Martin's.

APPENDIX A: WHICH SHAPE ARE YOU?

(Excerpt from "Soft Skills" published by the USDL, Office of Disability Employment Policy)

The "Which Shape Are You" test posits that there are five basic personality types, and each type tends to prefer a different shape. Following are the descriptions that the USDL provides for each shape. Take a look at these definitions and think about how closely they represent your individual personality.

According to the USDL:

- If you are a SQUARE: You are an organized, logical, and hardworking person who likes structure and rules. But sometimes you have trouble making decisions because you always want more information. You feel most comfortable in a stable environment with clear directions on what to do. You tend to like things that are regular and orderly. You will work on a task until it is finished, no matter what.

- If you are a RECTANGLE: You are a courageous (brave), exciting, and inquisitive explorer who always searches for ways to grow and change. You enjoy trying things you've never done before and love asking questions that have never been asked. You like structure, and will often be the person to be sure things are done the proper way, taking all rules and regulations into consideration. When you are given a task you will start organizing it to be sure it can be done in the most systematic way.

- If you are a TRIANGLE: You are a born leader who's competitive, confident, and can make decisions. You also like recognition. You are goal oriented and enjoy planning something out and then doing it (you are motivated by the accomplishment). You will tend to look at big long-term issues, but might forget the details. When given a task you set a goal and work on a plan for it. American business has traditionally been run by triangles and, although usually men, more women are taking those roles today.

- If you are a CIRCLE: You are social and communicative. There are no hard edges about you. You handle things by talking about them and smoothing things out with everybody. Communication is your first priority. When given a task, you will want to talk about it. You are a "people person," with lots of sympathy and consideration for others. You listen and communicate well and are very perceptive about other people's feelings. You like harmony and hate making unpopular decisions.

- If you are a SQUIGGLE: You are "off-the-wall" and creative. You like doing new and different things most of the time and get bored with regularity. When given a task, you will come up with bright ideas about how to do it. But you don't think in a deliberate pattern from A to B to C. Instead, you tend to jump around in your mind, going from A to M to X.

Like any personality test, the "Which Shape Are You?" test is limited in the amount of information it can provide to an individual. So, while we are hesitant to subscribe to the results of simple personality tests, it is nevertheless interesting to see if the shapes that attract us have any relationship to our behaviors or work styles in a group. What we find more interesting about this activity is the various ways team members interpret the meanings of the shapes they have selected.

APPENDIX B: PRE-CONTRACT TEAMWORK QUESTIONNAIRE

Q1 When I am working on a project on my own, I tend to ... (select all that apply)

- plan ahead and get assignments done early
- ask questions of the instructor and my classmates
- spend a lot of time preparing before I write
- jump right into the project and figure it out as I go
- procrastinate and then scramble to get the project done at the last minute

Q2 When I am working on a project in a group, I tend to ... (select one answer)

- jump in and take the lead by planning or organizing the team's work
- wait to see how others want to approach the work then offer my ideas
- analyze the project first and then try to figure out the best way to approach it
- make sure that everyone on the team is happy with the approach we are taking

Q3 For me, the best part of working on a team is
(fill in the blank): _____

Q4 My biggest concern or pet peeve about other team members is when they ... (select one answer):

- insist on their way or no way
- only give negative criticism
- dominate a meeting
- refuse to participate or contribute ideas

- cannot focus on task or gets off task easily
- show disinterest by focusing on their phones/social media
- interrupt with incessant questions
- being overly deferential to avoid conflict
- do not meet deadlines
- submit subpar work that fails to adhere to the grading criteria

Q5   I prefer to use these communication methods or productivity tools for group projects … (select all that apply):

- Emailing drafts back and forth
- Texting via phone number
- Texting via apps like Whatsapp
- Face-to-face meetings

Q6   I am most proud of my ability to … (select one answer):

- lead or manage a project
- research (e.g., using the library database)
- use text or design tools such as Google Docs, Microsoft Word, Microsoft Excel effectively
- write
- edit or revise
- analyze data/numbers

Q7   When writing a major paper or report as a group, I prefer to … (select one answer):

- "divide and conquer" by assigning different parts to different members so that each member can work at his/her own time/pace
- work virtually through tools (e.g., emails, Google Docs) and have everyone contribute to the same document asynchronously
- work virtually through tools (e.g., emails, Google Docs) and have everyone contribute to the same document synchronously

Q8   How do you prefer to solve a disagreement between team members (fill in the blank)? _____

Q9   I relate most strongly to someone who is … (select one answer):

- people-oriented
- results-oriented
- process-oriented

INDEX

Printed in the United States
by Baker & Taylor Publisher Services